THE RIGHT WAY
TO DRAW THE GREAT
OUTDOORS

Mark Linley

RIGHT WAY

Typeset in 12/14pt Cantoria by Letterpart Ltd., Reigate, Surrey.

Printed and bound in Great Britain by Guernsey Press Co. Ltd., Guernsey, Channel Islands, UK.

The *Right Way* series is published by Elliot Right Way Books, Brighton Road, Lower Kingswood, Tadworth, Surrey, KT20 6TD, U.K. For information about our company and the other books we publish, visit our website at www.right-way.co.uk

CONTENTS

INTRODUCTION   5

Chapter 1   Beginning to Draw Animals   7
Chapter 2   Raining Cats and Dogs   12
Chapter 3   Rabbits and Other Rodents   22
Chapter 4   Wildlife in Your Back Yard   31
Chapter 5   Dear Deer   38
Chapter 6   Gee Up   43
Chapter 7   Down on the Farm   48
Chapter 8   Feathered Friends   55
Chapter 9   Odds and Ends   62
Chapter 10   Beginning to Draw Flowers   69
Chapter 11   A Wild Bunch   75
Chapter 12   An English Country Garden   80
Chapter 13   Go Potty   84
Chapter 14   Easy Landscapes   88
Chapter 15   Don't Rush Your Bridges   94
Chapter 16   Tangle with Timber   98
Chapter 17   Take to the Hills   103
Chapter 18   Buildings in Landscapes   110
Chapter 19   Tricks of the Trade   114
Chapter 20   Out and About   122

By the same author:

The Right Way to Draw
The Right Way to Draw People: Including Cartoons and Caricatures

Uniform with this book

INTRODUCTION

We love the Great Outdoors
This book is a complete course for beginner artists who want to learn how to draw outdoor pictures, such as animals, flowers and landscapes. Step-by-step instructions are given for most of the drawings used as examples within these pages. You will start each section with easy studies which have been created to boost your self-confidence, and to show you that *anyone* can learn this skill. If you have never drawn anything except breath, don't worry: I have ways of teaching you!

At first glance, the sketch on the right might seem difficult to do. Actually, this type of drawing is quite easy — once you have gained the necessary know-how about shading. By working through this book you will achieve a high standard of draftsmanship. You will feel justifiably pleased. Indeed, by purchasing this book you have already proved that you *want* to learn *The Right Way to Draw the Great Outdoors*. So even before you put pencil or pen to paper you are half way there. Well done!

People who want to draw nature tend to have a deep regard for wildlife and our vanishing countryside. Naturally they wish to record what they see for posterity. I earnestly hope this book will help them.

How to top up your confidence
If you have already read any other of my books (listed on page 4 of this one) you will know how positive thinking will transform your drawing. The following paragraph summarises this for new readers.

What is confidence? My dictionary defines it thus: a firm trust, a feeling of reliance or certainty, sense of self-reliance, boldness.

This quality is indispensable for success in any field, but how do you achieve it at once? Very easily! You start to think and act positively. How? Simple! You decide you *can* draw. How does that work? Your conscious thought instructs your wonderful personal computer (your sub-conscious mind) which immediately programs every brain cell towards achieving your object. Beware! When you think "I *can't* draw", your mind does the opposite. Your computer operates just as fast and powerfully on negative instructions!

Positive thinking works like magic. Try it from this moment on. Try it on all things in your life, not simply art.

What you will need

Now that you are brimming with confidence and enthusiasm, you can rush round to your local art shop for some tools of your new trade. Black-and-white drawings have a special charm and power. Indeed, before colour printing was invented, most illustrations were in this medium. Black ink and various nibs used to be common, but today artists use ready-made pens. All the drawings in this book were done with them. There is a huge range to choose from. I find that a small selection of pens, graded 0.1, 0.5 and 0.7, is more than adequate for most illustrations, and suggest that you purchase the same. Despite being 'throw away' pens they are made to give long service. One pen will contain enough black ink to make dozens of drawings and they are not expensive.

Draftsmen's pens are also very useful for the artist who produces many drawings. They come in many sizes and use an ink cartridge. Being technical pens they cost more, but with care will last for years. Both kinds are stocked by most good stationery and art material shops.

You will want to have a few soft pencils, 2B, 4B or 6B, as well, because all your early attempts should be lightly drawn in pencil first. A sharp blade is much better for keeping pencils in working order than a conventional sharpener. Artists cut a chisel point on their lead, making a thin but wide point. This will draw fine or thick lines, making your pencil into a double-purpose one. A medium-hard eraser will be handy for removing stubborn marks.

You will need an A4 size cartridge paper drawing pad, and a smaller A5 one for keeping in your pocket, handbag or car. An A5 pad was used to sketch from life many of the drawings used in these pages. A supply of good-quality typing paper is wonderful for rough sketches and can also be used for final work. This is far cheaper than cartridge paper, especially when you purchase it by the ream (500 sheets). For pen work a smooth surfaced paper is helpful.

A small good-quality paintbrush (number 3, 4 or 5) and a bottle of black drawing ink may be handy for blocking in large areas or for creating silhouettes.

Many would-be artists believe that drawing animals is a particularly difficult skill. It is not! The secrets in this art medium are knowing how to go about it, and being confident. Don't worry. I will give you confidence and teach, in easy stages, how to draw animals superbly. I know that by purchasing this book you already have a deep interest in the natural world, so you are already well under way.

The drawings in this book have been designed so that you can copy them. As you become proficient you will then be able to draw animals from life. This, in fact, is still copying but it requires a little more self-confidence and accurate observation.

My life-long interest in animals began when I was just over four years old. The family lodge reflected hunting in South-East Asia during the days when wildlife abounded: the sightless gaze of deer and buffalo looked down at me from the walls; glass-eyed leopards' heads stared up from skins on floors; an elephant foot served as a plant pot holder. Wildlife pictures hung everywhere.

I was encouraged by my non-artistic father to draw live-looking animals from dead ones. My poor efforts were richly praised and as a result my self-confidence blossomed.

I had my first encounter with an exotic live animal a few years later. One day my eccentric father came across a sale of stock from a bankrupt circus. He disappeared inside a huge tent and shortly came out leading two llamas. They were to be pets for my brother and me. On that special day an enterprising newspaper man took a photograph of one bewildered small boy perched astride a frisky llama, to which he clung grimly. It was me — and the picture made the front page!

My father seemed not to have given much thought to the problems of keeping two large animals in the back garden of an average-sized semi-detached house. The llamas were taken by trailer to our home, however they soon had to be removed to a farm twenty-five miles away. I used to look forward to the weekends we visited our pets. A year or two later the gentle llamas, called Billy and Lady, were given to a zoo.

Now you know why I am interested in animals, why I'm a conservationist, and why I eventually became a wildlife artist.

A secret revealed

Finally, before you begin, I would like to share with you my big secret of how to draw animals accurately from life, especially when they are on the move: *look* at your subject for as long as you can. Ask yourself questions. What overall shape is the body? Is it long, curved, oblong or what? Next observe the head. Is it generally wedge-shaped, long, thin, oval or some other shape? Is the face deep, wide or chubby? Are the eyes forward facing? Are they in proportion? Does the animal have long legs, short or medium ones? What sort of feet does it have? Hooves or paws, with four or five claws?

An experienced artist will store a mental note of all this information in seconds. You may take a whole minute! However, you must concentrate on the basic *outline* — the silhouette shape — first above all. Instantly you have this fundamental information logged in your brain computer, start drawing. Stop looking at the animal. Jot down the bare body shape swiftly in the position you want — walking, feeding, or whatever. Add the neck and head in outline, and the legs and tail in proportion.

Is your silhouette right? Could a friend already recognise what the animal is at once? Go for it again if you need to. Because, no matter how brilliantly you may add smaller details, you will never capture the animal on paper if your fundamental outline misses the target! Shape up right and your genius will emerge!

Now flash your eyes back to your subject. This time you want to refresh your memory on the small details which you should have purposely waited to attack: you are checking the formation of paw, foot or claw; noting if the tail is spindly or bushy and whether the ears are long, short or folded flat; observing how nostrils, mouth and jaw come together, and so on. Finally, you can turn your attention to coat markings.

The message is that you can only ever successfully add bit by bit onto a soundly constructed basic shape. This applies equally to people, by the way, as much as it does to animals.

In order to teach myself how to draw animals I spent many hours observing and sketching in zoos, wildlife parks and natural history museums. You can learn my skills without doing this. Most of the creatures used as examples in this book are common to town and countryside.

The first animal artists

The simple but accurate drawings of the world's first animal artists are still on the cave walls on which they were drawn many thousands of years ago. They will probably remain as long as our planet survives.

Early man had far less intelligence and a smaller brain than ours, so how, then, could he draw the animals around him? Those cavemen who were perhaps instinctively artistic had the ability to make good observations. It was important to them to be able to show others of their tribe what sort of animals were available for food.

Looking properly is vital to all drawing. I do not think that early man was gifted. Drawing is a skill rather than a gift, although all professions produce the occasional genius. Early man knew how to *look* — the secret of being able to draw!

Cavemen drew with charcoal (burnt wood), coloured clay, earth and lamp black from their hollowed-out stone lamps. The home-made paint or ink was applied with hands, fingers or a stick. Think of all the advantages you start with!

Be an Ice Age artist

Ice Age artists left behind many examples of their work, some of which were very advanced. The bison was one of their most popular subjects. They hunted this beast for food. It was often drawn in black paint. A few excellent clay models have been found.

The sketch below shows an Ice Age type drawing of a bison. I have drawn this in easy stages. The upper illustration is of the general basic shape. The one below shows how a few details have been added, with the final sketch at the bottom of the page. Notice how few lines there seem to be. I want you to copy this illustration.

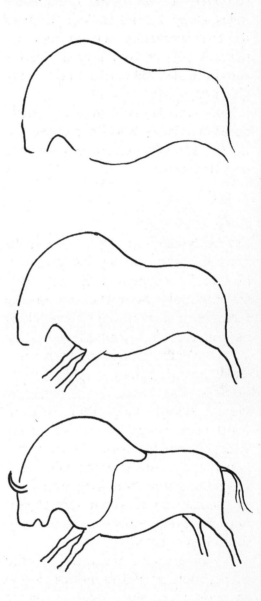

First, sharpen your 2B pencil into a chisel point. This is done with a sharp blade. The lead should be made into a wedge shape so that it has a wide edge and also a thin side when turned — a chisel point, as below. This is very useful because you have a dual purpose pencil which will give a broad or thin line.

The animal shown below is called an ibex. It's a goat-like creature which inhabits remote mountainous regions in Europe. The ibex was once very plentiful but is now only found in small numbers.

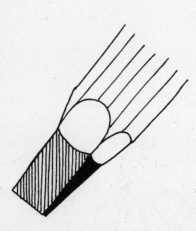

Don't worry about the fact of merely copying at this stage; pretty well all beginner artists start this way. It's useful because it teaches observation and gives help with different techniques.

Now continue your work by taking a long look at the sketch on the right of this page. Then, with the same pencil, lightly put down the essential lines as you tackle it. When you are happy with the drawing, ink over it using your size 0.1 pen. When it is dry (about one minute) erase only the pencil lines which still show, and admire your handiwork!

Take a look at the overall shape of the animal, then try to sketch it quickly and boldly. Remember that once you get the basic shape right you will have a correct structure on which to work. Adding the details of the eye and horn markings will then be quite easy.

Now sketch the Ice Age horse below in the same way. Notice how the use of so few bold lines by early artists did not detract from the power and accuracy of their work.

Points to note
1. You can draw better than cave-men.
2. Be bold, confident and enthusiastic.
3. Expect mistakes — they are normal.

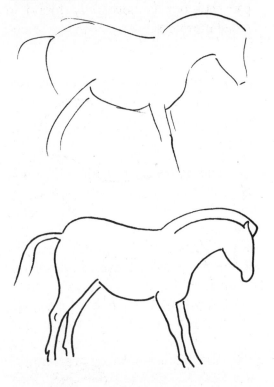

In France and Spain there are some remarkable cave drawings of prehistoric horses. These stocky animals had stiff manes and short legs.

Ice Age artists portrayed many other kinds of animal. The mammoth, which we tend to think of as a huge hairy elephant, was smaller than our jumbo of today. Foxes, wolves, bears, lions and reindeer were immortalised on cave walls.

CHAPTER 2
RAINING CATS AND DOGS

Get up to scratch with cats

First, I'm gong to teach you how to draw the type of cat found in every village, town and city in England: the short-haired domestic moggy, who is also popular the world over. If you can sketch a cat accurately, then you will be able to draw any creature. It is the pet most frequently drawn by beginner artists. We shall spend extra time learning how to depict this fascinating animal.

Cats of all kinds are my favourite subjects. I like to watch them, stroke them, draw, paint and sculpt them. The graceful way they move gives an impression of hidden power. A flexible coat and spine allows them to adopt a wide range of interesting poses.

When you can correctly draw a cat's face you have solved the hardest part of the job. Many people go wrong here because a cat's skull structure is not easy to fathom at first glance. The bone formation resembles a lop-sided plum pudding with eyes and ears. Don't worry — you are about to bring your cats up to scratch!

Unlike dogs, all cats have a similar face. Once you can draw cats you should be capable of portraying their big relations: tigers, lions, leopards and right through the other 37 species of the feline family!

My Top Cat

Like millions of other people I have a pet cat. She adopted me when she was a five month old stray kitten. She knew a mug when she saw one! It is likely that our domestic cat is descended from ancestors who lived in ancient Egypt 4,000 years ago. Cats were then deemed to be gods and treated as such. My own pet seems aware of this, judging by the way she demands instant attention and easily manipulates me into obtaining exactly what she wants.

I have reminded her that, in Medieval days, the Church, quite wickedly, pronounced all cats to be devils. My moggy dismissed this bit of history with an imperious look and an angry twitch of her tail. She probably knew that, as a result of a Papal decree, cats were cruelly persecuted for years; this happened despite cats being worth their weight in gold during the Great Plague, which was caused by millions of rats. I call my pet TC, Top Cat. We shall use her as a model for many of the exercises that follow.

Below are some quick sketches of TC. Examine the two profiles. The 3-dimensional feel is achieved by adding fur sparingly, first put in with dotted lines. Copy these sketches carefully — they hold the key to drawing all cats well.

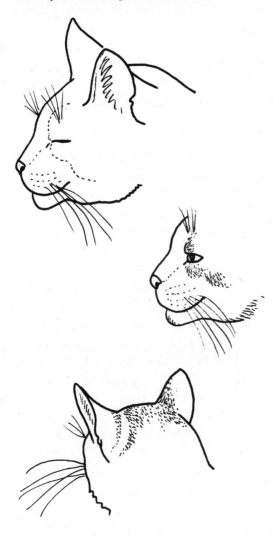

Observe how small and delicate the nose is and how cats always seem to be smiling, due to a gently curved mouth line. The lower jaw fits snugly into the top jaw.

See the way the ears have been drawn. A cat's ear has a thick ridge round the base at the rear, as shown in the lower illustration.

Most cats have white whiskers, but you can depict these with fine black lines. There are a group of six whiskers over each eye, and four or five rows on each side of the mouth. You don't have to put them all in — a few will do.

My cat has a pronounced forehead. This feature varies slightly from cat to cat, as does the length of the nose. In this respect, animal faces are like human faces. Every one is unique. TC has a short nose. She was having a cat nap when I first sketched her, so her eyes were closed. In my second profile you can see TC doesn't miss a trick when her eyes are open! Cats, by the way, spend three quarters of their lives asleep or resting. This is good for us artists!

To begin with, leave out detailed fur. I return to help you with that shortly. You will also help yourself by making all your drawings larger than the printed versions in this book.

Drawing a cat's face from the front should not give you any more trouble than a profile sketch — once you learn where each feature should go. The most common errors I see beginners make include drawing the cat's nose too big and the ears perfectly triangular, which they are not. In fact, they are petal-like in structure with curved ends. There is a small kink at the outer rim.

Newcomers to art tend to draw a cat's eyes too large and too high in the face. There is black skin round a cat's eyes. We normally see the bottom half of this. The top half is usually covered by a fold of skin — a cat's eyelid. However, in a drawing, little more than the outline shape of the eye is enough to portray without excess detail intruding.

Practise drawing some more cat heads from life, from books or from your photo album until you can do them from memory. This will be a big advance for you.

Let sleeping cats lie

Study the sketch above. Notice that the basic shape is oval. The ears are elliptical. Roughly half way between ear tips and bottom of the lower jaw is where the eyes look out. Half way between the eyebrows and lower jaw line is where the *top* of the nose is. With a little practice you will soon automatically get these proportions right. Copy this example in pencil; then ink it in.

The sketches above show TC in three sleeping positions. See how her legs have been drawn. Redraw these, twice the size, using pen or pencil.

When you are able to draw a sleeping cat accurately you will then be able to draw one in any position. A sleeping moggy may be deep in dreamland and appear to be motionless, but no sooner do you start sketching than she will suddenly twitch, stretch, and assume a different position! A cat resting, however, will normally remain in the same pose for a long time.

The secret is to observe carefully and then quickly jot down the basic shape. After that it doesn't matter if the cat moves because you can take your time adding the little details.

When drawing cats, put coat markings in last. Remember how to convey the curve of body, muscle and limb, by the way you make your marks on the paper. TC is a multi-coloured tortoiseshell cat.

With most modern drawing pens you can work very fast. The ink will not smudge easily. You can produce an excellent pencil drawing by using a hard pencil (H) for the outline, then a soft one (4B) to give middle tones and deep shades. Beautiful pencil drawings are quite rare. Don't ignore this medium which, in fact, is easier than pen work.

Watching the watcher
As mentioned previously, cats spend much of their time resting. TC, for example, will stay in a comfortable position for ages if she is watching her territory from the vantage point of a window-sill inside the kitchen.

This drawing will show you how I have depicted TC's fur markings. Study the way I have used fine lines, dots and dashes to give an illusion of different colours and tones. Copy this. If your drawing goes wrong, don't worry. Look again and then re-draw. Be determined — and patient!

This sketch gives the rounded basic shapes which combine to make up the outline drawing. Try filling in the fur details.

15

This illustration shows TC when she looks round to see what I'm up to. Copy this in pencil or pen.

A friend's pet was used as a model for the sketch below. She has very dark markings along her back, her stripes are black and her face and chest are white. Draw your version of this tabby cat. Although you are copying my work your efforts will not be exactly like mine. This is good because you are developing your own unique style. You could become the best cat artist in the world!

Clean cats

Cats spend a good deal of their time grooming. They are one of the cleanest animals around. They always follow the same procedure when having a wash and brush up: they begin with their paws; then comes the head, followed by flanks, body and the tail last of all. During their ablutions they make many interesting shapes.

Above are some grooming positions. Draw a page or two of these, and have a shot at putting in the markings as I have done in the upper sketch. Make your studies larger than mine.

Moving moggies

Moggies on the move are graceful creatures. At times they go like lightning, much too fast for our eyes to see.

The sketch above was drawn when I saw a little tiger visiting in my garden. See, *as always*, how the basic shape was first jotted down before finishing the drawing. The stripes were put in with a size 0.5 pen. All the tiny dots were drawn with a 0.1 pen.

My moggy seems to hate others of her kind, though she likes people. She will normally attack any moggy who enters her territory. The battle is usually short and sharp. Fur flies everywhere, but it isn't hers! I once watched her as she confronted a fox who trotted down the garden path. She transformed herself by puffing out her fur. Her tail closely resembled that of the fox. She hissed loudly. The fox cautiously walked round her then went on its way.

Above is my impression of an angry cat. See how you get on with copying this one.

Kittens

Kittens, like all baby animals, have a lot of appeal and are very popular subjects with the buying public. Kittens seem to have huge ears. This is because they grow slower from birth than the rest of the head and it seems to be nature's way for them to start proportionally larger.

Tackle the portrait of the long-haired kitten below next. Notice the large eyes and ears. The long fur is best drawn with quick, loose strokes. Try it.

Have a look at the cute kitten above. Build a basic shape from this, then make a finished drawing. It should be good enough to make a little present for your favourite cat person.

Woof woof

Dogs are unique animals. All they seem to want from us is love, affection, food and shelter. While millions of people keep dogs, there are many owners who do not understand dog behaviour. Folk do not realise that this popular creature has strong pack instincts. If the owner is not the pack leader then the dog will take over this role with sometimes disastrous consequences. The modern trend towards keeping potentially lethal guard dogs all too often proves this point.

Most household pets, however, are delightful little chums who are faithful, loyal, good company and fun.

Unlike domestic cats, dogs come in all shapes and sizes. All dogs do not share the same type of skull. Some have deep foreheads while others are streamlined, stubby, long or whatever. There are so many different breeds that I can cover only a few of them.

Start with heads

One of my favourite dogs is the Border Collie. This wonderful sheep controller is very popular and has been made more so by television series which feature sheep dog trials. I once owned a city-bred Collie, who was a great pet but not trained to round up anything other than me! He was full of energy, very friendly and good to be with.

Look at my drawings of two adult dogs and a puppy above. Notice the well-defined foreheads and the long snouts. I have left a white line around part of the ears so their shape can be seen. The black markings, which are quite black on these animals, were put in with a brush and black drawing ink. Copy the sketches by starting with the construction lines, as shown; then the little details added in become easy.

The front views of the heads below are slightly more difficult but not beyond your talent. See how the eyes are drawn between the dotted lines. If you use a pencil for the basic sketch this will help you to produce an accurate illustration quickly. Use dot stipple and tiny lines to depict fur.

A bit of action
The Collie seems to control sheep fully by simply fixing his eyes on them. The sheep immediately look worried but do exactly what the shepherd and the dog want — if they both know their jobs

I have drawn Border Collies stalking and dashing after sheep for the illustration above. The sketches were done after first drawing several quick pencil roughs then working on the best of them with a pen. Try this system when you copy these drawings.

Another dog seen on television in trials is the Cocker Spaniel, who excels in scenting out and retrieving game birds. They are intelligent, obedient creatures who make good pets when not plunging through undergrowth.

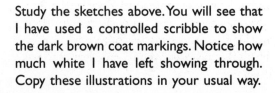

Study the sketches above. You will see that I have used a controlled scribble to show the dark brown coat markings. Notice how much white I have left showing through. Copy these illustrations in your usual way.

Assignments
1. From life or photographs, draw three different cats.
2. Watch a cat for a while. Then look down at your drawing pad and capture the outline shape with deft strokes. Check your effort by looking at your subject again. Now tackle detail such as face, tail and claws. You can sneak another look whenever necessary. Finally, draw the fur markings.
3. Try to sketch three different breeds of dog. Work from life or photographs.
4. Draw your past impressions of a dog moving. Use pencil or pen.

CHAPTER 3
RABBITS AND OTHER RODENTS

Rabbit, rabbit, rabbit
Rabbits, bless them, are delightful animals, common throughout the English countryside. It is just as well for them that they breed so freely. Little bunnies provide tasty snacks for foxes, weasels, stoats and birds of prey. In additional to its natural enemies, the species is constantly persecuted by man. It remains, nevertheless, a much loved animal by children and many adults.

It's all in the head
After your work in the last chapter, you will find that rabbits are much easier to sketch than are cats and dogs. Once again, the most common error made by beginner artists is in portraying the head. There is an easy way of drawing this correctly. When you can draw a rabbit's head shape accurately you will be well on the way to sketching all animals that have a similar skull shape: hares, squirrels, mice and other common rodents.

Look at the illustration below. The top sketch shows a rough pear-like form. The middle illustration has this shape more clearly defined by four straight lines of different lengths. This is the correct format for a rabbit's skull. Fix this in your mind. Then draw it from memory. The lower drawing has been completed by added details. The straight lines are now not quite so straight. See how the eye, nostril, petal-like ears, fur and whiskers have been depicted. I used a size 0.1 pen for this. Copy this in either pen or pencil.

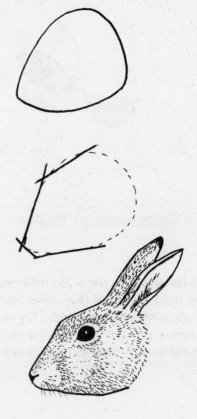

Start with the young
Young rabbits are easy to draw. They have oval bodies, small ears and heads like those you have just drawn. When rabbits are very small they seem to be happy creatures, unafraid of man. By keeping still you can observe them at close quarters for long periods of time.

You can create fur texture by putting in dot stipple with a size 0.1 pen. The best way of doing this is to hold your pen in a relaxed grip and bump it quickly up and down on the paper. You simply do more dots where you want the deepest tone or shadow, and few where you want white or reflected light to show.

You can get a good picture in pencil alone with the advantage that a background tone is possible. Use a grade HB for the outline then a 2B for putting in background tone. The tone is done by *rubbing* the 2B lead on to a piece of scrap paper, covering an area of, say, a postcard, and then taking it off with a bit of clean cloth which you use to transfer it onto the area you wish to cover. This avoids having any pencil strokes showing. Once you add your dot stipple with an HB pencil to achieve the look of real fur, with dots, short dashes and lines, the resulting bunny will look more realistic than a pen sketch. By using two or more pencil grades a wide range of tones is possible. This simple technique can be applied to all animal subjects and to many landscape backgrounds.

This was drawn to show you how to make the basic outlines and then go on to finish your drawings of young rabbits. Try copying the above in pencil and pen. Notice how the head outline slightly overlaps the body oval.

Your next task is to work out the basic outlines of the rabbits drawn below. Use a larger scale than used here. (How to enlarge drawings is dealt with in Chapter 9.) When you have done this, put in all the details. Work in pen, pencil or both.

and is black on the top and a pure white underneath. (This is used as a warning sign to others of its kind.) Rabbits are rather cat-like in the way they groom themselves, sit, rest, and are given to sudden bursts of fast movement.

Adult rabbits

As a rabbit grows to become an adult, some features naturally change from those it had as a kitten (the correct term for a baby bunny). We need to be acutely aware of these differences when drawing them. The hind legs are larger and more powerful; the ears are longer and usually black-tipped; the tail is slightly bigger

Study the drawings above and then copy them. First draw the basic shapes before progressing to the finished illustrations.

A rabbit bolting from danger moves very quickly. Its head is held backwards with ears laid low along the rabbit's back. The tail is high to signal possible impending disaster. You can see what the legs do by looking at the sketch below. Copy this example to a larger scale; then put in fur detail.

I watched rabbits of all ages enjoying a Spring afternoon. Some were feeding, others grooming; a few loped about whilst comrades rested or slept. Accurate basic outlines were what I wanted. No details were drawn at this stage. Close-up views were obtained by squinting through lightweight binoculars. In less than an hour I had more than enough rabbit shapes to work from. Next time you visit rabbit territory take a small drawing pad and do the same exercise.

Draw rabbits from life

The very best way of learning how to draw is to get out, observe, then quickly jot down what you see on your sketch pad. Almost all the rabbit drawings in this chapter are from sketches that I made on one trip to the countryside. I found a large field which was enclosed by tough wire mesh fencing used to safeguard petrol storage tanks. The place was a haven for rabbits. Their enemies could not easily get at them.

These are rabbit outlines. Draw a few or all of these to a larger scale. Then put in fur texture using the techniques I have given you.

25

The handsome hare

The hare is very similar in structure to a rabbit. It has the same sort of skull shape with longer hind legs and ears. You may have seen these handsome animals boxing each other, balancing on their hind legs. This is a courting routine that begins in early spring and can continue for several months. Hares are found in pastures and where there is hilly meadow land.

A hare will always try to escape danger by galloping up a hill rather than down. The sketch above of a hare in flight will give you the idea of how to draw it in action. Have a go at this but make it bigger than the printed version. Draw in some fur detail.

This should show you how to draw the head and body of a hare. There are no new problems for you with these. Draw them in pencil or ink.

Little furry friends

You will learn quickly how to draw some of our smaller furry friends, as they have a similar head structure to a rabbit.

I paid a visit to a pet shop in order to buy wild bird food but I was distracted for some time by the antics of caged hamsters and gerbils. I asked the proprietor if he would mind me drawing his small charges. He was delighted to know that his animals would appear in this book. It is always wise first to obtain an owner's permission to sketch the creature you want as a subject.

Draw a busy hamster

Inside the pet shop my observations began with a group of hamsters. This charming short-lived animal is a popular pet in schools and homes. The domesticated species are thought to have descended from a pair taken from the wild in a Far East country.

When not asleep, hamsters are very busy little animals that seem to hurtle about at high speed. Their tiny hands and feet have five fingers or toes. Sometimes only four are visible.

After I had studied their basic shape and noted their fur texture I fixed these in my mind, then jotted down in pencil the outlines of various poses. Details were only put in when I was satisfied with the preliminary drawings. I always work through this method when sketching animals, birds, reptiles and people! I make no apology for repeating here the crucial importance of going for outlines and proportions first.

The picture on the right should show you how my technique works.

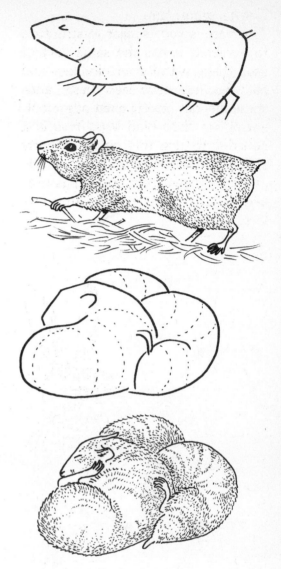

The upper sketch is a hamster gathering material for its nest. Notice how the body has a big end, and how alike the skull shape is to that of a rabbit. Don't forget the stumpy tail! The lower sketch depicts a ball of sleeping hamsters. I have used dotted lines, again, to help suggest body form at the outline stage. Hamsters have very short hair which has been suggested by tiny pen strokes and dots. Copy this in pencil, then in pen.

A hamster feeding was drawn for the illustration below. It appeared to be in a hurry to eat. After swiftly filling its cheek pouches with grain it scurried away onto the next project — hanging upside down from the cage roof. I used a grade 4B pencil for the basic outline then finished the job with a size 0.1 pen. Draw your version of this example.

lively day and night. As usual I had a long careful look at the gerbils before doing any drawing. This is vital preparation before art work can begin — especially when tackling fast moving creatures. Before I began to draw I knew what shape the body, head, legs, tail and ears were. I noted how their long, straggly fur grew, that they had bright eyes, and the most delicate little hands. This system works for me and it will work for you.

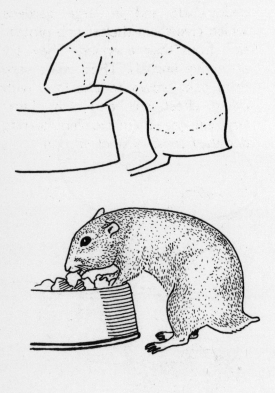

Draw a gerbil

My next captive subjects were gerbils. These long-haired mouse-like animals are just as active as hamsters. The wild gerbil is a desert rodent that is nocturnal. Pet gerbils seem to be

Study the illustration above for as long as you want. Without looking at it further, jot down the basic outline. Look again, then draw in the missing details.

Now repeat the exercise with the gerbils drawn for the illustration below.

Lock up the cat
My house was previously owned by a young lady who kept a dog. Consequently there were no cats about the garden, but there were delightful little wood mice. I first saw one of these animals when I put up a bird table. It popped out to sniff at my shoes. My cat watched it from the comfort of my garden chair. She did not budge! Kittens who have been taken away from their mothers too early have not been taught to hunt. At this time TC had no idea how to catch her natural lunch,

thank goodness. I was able to watch wood mice for several weeks before they were frightened away by numerous cats who soon invaded the garden when TC wasn't around to drive them off. My cat is the undefeated middleweight champion of the area!

Wood mice are common in the countryside and in large gardens which give them shelter and protection from their enemies. They are attractive animals. Their coats vary from pale brown to chestnut with cream chest, chin and belly. Their large ears give them excellent hearing and their sense of smell is good.

This is a pose typical of the wood mouse. Notice the oval body shape and a head that is rabbit-like. The long tail is hairless. This is another small friend with tiny fingers and toes. Copy this example in pencil or pen.

The illustrations below give other typical mouse positions. Have a go at drawing them. Pencil will be better than pen for depicting the fur texture. Remember to leave a white spot in the eye in order to give it a life-like look, and to put in a few whiskers.

During my schooldays I kept almost anything that moved as a pet. White mice were popular then. These and house mice are very similar to wood mice, except for the colour. I can recall, when working in an office years ago, finding a house mouse in a desk drawer where it had made a nest in old files. I fed the mouse on biscuit and bits of sandwich. It soon became tame. I used to look forward to our morning meetings. Then someone reported the matter to Pest Control. Office mice have a hard and short life!

Assignments

1. Choose a drawing of a rabbit from the outline drawings on page 25. Look at it for one minute. Close the book and draw it from memory. Check your work. Repeat this exercise with several more poses. This is wonderful practice for becoming good at drawing from life.
2. Draw a life-sized portrait of a rabbit from a photograph or from life.
3. Look at the hamster on page 28 again. Close the book and then draw what you studied. Your second attempt should be better than your first.
4. Draw a page full of mice.

CHAPTER 4
WILDLIFE IN YOUR BACK YARD

Be foxy

I live in a large city, yet the wild animal I most frequently see is the fox. This elegant, intelligent creature has been around man since the Stone Age. Thousands of years ago it learned that, where man was, there were likely to be free meals available. Today, as never before, the wily fox has established itself in every town and city. In an urban environment it is safe from the hunt, but victim of the motorist. Many are killed on our roads.

Shortly after I took up residence in my house, three fox cubs and their parents began to use my garden as a shortcut to their earth, which was under a tumbledown shed next door. Beyond the end of my patch there are neglected gardens which are covered in brambles and sprouting ash trees. It is a paradise for foxes. I have been able to study and sketch them almost daily.

Draw a portrait of Reynard

The fox got the name Reynard many hundreds of years ago. The name derives from *renard*, the French word for fox, and means 'unconquerable through his cleverness'. It is a very apt title for this resourceful animal which has an ultra-sensitive sense of smell, keen hearing and excellent vision. Farmers hate them because they kill their livestock, but lots of people admire them.

I have included the sketch above to show how to draw a profile of a fox. Notice the large elliptical ears which have a small kink in the outer rim, similar to that of a cat. The fox has a long pointed snout, large nose, and flared cheeks of white hair. The mask-like face is made more distinctive by dark tear-like marks from the corners of the eyes. This animal is a member of the dog family, but it is like a cat in its agility. Copy this sketch in pencil.

31

The hardest problem you have in drawing a fox is getting the head to look right. This, of course, is true of most animals.

City-bred cubs and vixens (females) do not seem to have a fear of man like that of a country fox. Those that live in my neck of the woods will let me approach quite near before moving off.

Easy poses

On most sunny Spring and Summer mornings I can look out of a bedroom window and see a fox or two basking on a shed roof. They like the sun and will curl up for long spells to sleep in its warmth. Sometimes I have crept slowly and quietly down the garden to get a close up sketch of a sleeping fox, but the fox has a sixth sense. The closed eyes suddenly spring open; it becomes fully alert and ready to disappear quickly.

This is what you see when a fox looks at you. A frontal view clearly shows the marvellous white fringe round the face. Copy this example in pen or pencil.

Look at the sketch above to see how the basic outline of a sleeping fox is turned into a finished sketch. Lots of dots and dashes again feature. Copy this as best you can.

Look at the example below. This is the view I often get when fox watching. Draw your own version.

The snout is short and the ears have yet to develop. The tail is short and stubby. Your town or city, like mine, may have a Nature Centre that has foxes. You might be able to sketch them from life as I do.

Chubby cubs

In November and December the nights become noisy with the blood-curdling screams of foxes. It is mating time. The cubs are born in March or April, but it is usually late May before I see the current year's litter. The small chubby cubs are very playful. They indulge in mock fights and affectionately groom each other. When young their fur seems spiky, fine and dark in colour.

Copy the sketches above. You will have to go dotty again to draw cubs. Hold your pen lightly so that it just touches the surface of your paper. It takes time but will keep you off the streets!

Hunter and scrounger

The fox is highly intelligent and is a great survivor. Its wonderful nose can soon pinpoint a food supply, whether it is a fat field mouse, a bird, or a turkey carcass in a dustbin. During the worst of winter, foxes can be seen tipping bins over to rake out anything edible. At dawn I have watched a dog fox nip under the gate of a Primary School, cross a playground, and inspect a row of bins. Litter louts who leave a trail of chips, fish remains, curry and other food about the streets provide the fox with supper. Foxes eat vegetables as well as meat.

I don't regularly feed foxes because they quickly take advantage of the situation. After I put out free meals for them a family of foxes began to visit my garden frequently. They dug holes everywhere. The vixen would sit and stare through the kitchen window. It was very interesting, but I also had to consider the safety of my cat, TC. She is young and takes care of herself, but there is evidence that cats who are old, weak or injured are eaten by foxes. I have noted that stray cats tend to disappear when there are growing fox cubs about.

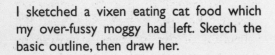

I sketched a vixen eating cat food which my over-fussy moggy had left. Sketch the basic outline, then draw her.

Have a look at my drawing of a fox hunting in my garden, above. Copy this. By now you should be quite good, if not brilliant, at animal drawing. It will help you to look back at your early efforts to see how you have improved.

Bright-eyed and bushy-tailed

The grey squirrel, like the fox, is another wild animal which has taken to our towns in a big way. It is an intelligent, attractive creature which is also a great pest. Despite man, it is a resourceful survivor found in many of our parks, woods and cities.

The grey squirrel was introduced to England a few hundred years ago from North America. It quickly spread throughout the country and was thought to have displaced the native red squirrel. Today this theory is no longer acknowledged by experts. They now think that the red squirrel has become rare because its habitat has shrunk, which is a much more likely explanation.

Just round the corner from where I live there is a busy main road which is lined by tall trees. Grey squirrels build their nests, or drays, in these on a level with the buses' upper deck passengers! If folk are observant they can watch them while on their way to work.

Draw cheeky chops

Grey squirrels frequently pay a visit to my garden to raid the bird food or dig up newly planted flower beds. My cat used to chase them into a nearby rowan tree. For a long time the squirrels could always out-climb the cat, but one day she managed to corner a young squirrel in my neighbour's porch. I thought that she would kill the youngster, but all she wanted to do was sniff noses with him. From then on the mad pursuit stopped!

Observe how similar the head shape of a squirrel, which is a rodent, is to that of a mouse or rabbit. See also the way I have suggested the tail by drawing longish pen strokes which generally radiate around the tail itself. I have left white space in abundance at the back of the tail. I used short lines to suggest body fur texture. Copy the basic outline first and then draw meticulously in pencil or pen. You might try drawing the tree branch. See how the roundness of this has been suggested by short, curved pen strokes. It's easy!

35

Changing shapes

The grey squirrel, like so many animals, can suddenly change shape dramatically. It is a very agile creature which can climb and bound across open ground at great speed. Squirrels are often filmed overcoming one obstacle after another in order to get to food. One little fellow who visited my garden showed the same sort of intelligence. I had hung a box of peanuts on a clothes line for the birds. The squirrel bit through the line then took his time to eat the spilled nuts. This happened twice more before I put one up attached by a wire line. Did I win? No!

The squirrel sketched below is in a common pose, sitting up to eat. See how I have drawn the animal and the branch upon which its sits. Copy this example in pencil or pen.

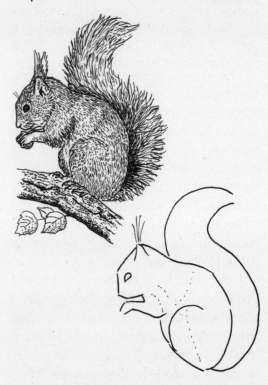

Notice the flowing lines made by tail and body and how the head is angled out. Copy this one.

The rare red squirrel

A few people are lucky enough to have the rare red squirrel as a garden visitor but most of us would have to explore remote regions in order to see this pretty animal. The one time I have seen one in the wild was on a ramble through a beech wood in the Lake District. The red squirrel is unmistakable. It has a lovely red coat and long tufts of hair on its ears. It is an animal which is found more often in Scotland than in England, where it is confined to small regions of beech wood or coniferous forest. The red squirrel is smaller and slimmer than the chubby grey one. It also has longer fur.

Squirrels are very nervous creatures which move rapidly. They spring from branch to branch before suddenly stopping to listen or look. The red squirrel's 'looking and listening' pose is sketched below. You can clearly see how the hair radiates from the central bone of the tail. This drawing is your next exercise, but scale it up larger than the printed version.

Assignments

1. Choose two foxy illustrations from this Chapter, then look at them for a minute. Close the book and draw them from memory, after first drawing a basic outline.
2. Go out and draw foxes from life — or through a bedroom window!
3. Draw a squirrel from a photograph. Include a bit of the background.
4. Observe and draw grey squirrels from life.

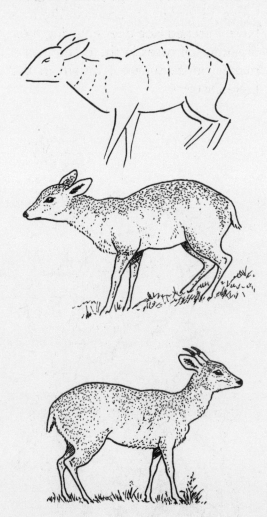

There are four species of deer which can be found in the wild in our country. We can see them in woodlands, on moors, and in the Scottish Highlands. Because their meat (venison) has become popular, Red deer are also found in deer farms in many parts of the country.

Deer are nervous, gentle creatures which are not too hard to draw once their basic construction is learnt. Deer tend to have powerful bodies supported by thin legs. The male animals grow antlers each year, spectacular by the time they are mature. They shed their antlers, usually in the late autumn, then re-grow another pair. They are larger than the females. Fallow deer are the most common deer. However, we shall start by learning how to draw the smallest deer, the Muntjac.

Muntjac deer

The lively, lovely little Muntjac deer is found in woodlands in the South, the Midlands, and the Chilterns. It originally escaped from Woburn Estates, and is slowly increasing its range. It is around 45 to 48cm tall at the shoulder. The buck (male) has two tiny antlers which are shed late in the year. The small size of the Muntjac makes it very vulnerable to marauding dogs.

The sketches above illustrate the basic form of both sexes of Muntjac deer. The top drawing is of the doe (female). I used very fine dot stipple to suggest the short hair. My size 0.1 pen was held very gently and just dabbed onto the paper for this result. A heavy hand or slow jabs do not work for this ultra-fine technique. Copy the examples but draw them out three times the size of the printed sketches.

Roe deer

The Roe deer is common in parts of the Midlands, the North, Scotland and across the South of England. It is about 20cm larger than the Muntjac. Deer tend to feed at dawn or dusk, so it is necessary to go out at these times in order to observe them. I have watched Roe deer enjoying their breakfast of roses in the gardens of a manor house where I taught in the Lake District.

This is my sketch of a buck Roe sniffing the morning air for his favourite snack. Notice the two small antlers. Draw your version of this deer.

Fallow deer

The Fallow deer is probably the most often seen of all deer species. These pretty animals can be observed in the grounds of stately homes, estates, parks, zoos, nature reserves and in woodlands of England, Wales and Ireland. If you visit Richmond Park you may never find any conkers on the ground, despite the many horse chestnut trees there are. The various deer there eat up every one that falls, including the prickles. They must have mouths as tough as my old walking boots!

The Fallow deer is a handsome animal, easily recognised by the buck's flattened antlers, called palmated because the shape originally reminded people of the palm of a man's hand. I once came across a buck which had shed one antler. The remaining one was dangling loose as the animal moved. I felt sure that I would soon own a souvenir of the woodlands so I trotted after the buck. After an exhausting half-hour the antler was still attached to the deer which then easily lost me. Many of the bucks have white spots on their reddish brown coats. Both sexes have a white patch on the rump, and a black or dark stripe down the centre of the short tail which is held upright as a warning when danger threatens. The Fallow doe has no antlers. She is plain but sweet.

Study the basic shapes on the left. Draw, in pencil, these construction lines. Remember that once you get the basic shape right the rest is very easy, so you will always end up with a reasonable drawing.

Now look at the finished sketches on the right. See how I have suggested the grain on the antlers, and the texture of the coat. I first pencilled in the spots so that I could ink in the fine lines and dots round them. Then the pencil marks were erased. Now finish off your sketch in a similar fashion.

A popular image
A young Fallow, Roe or Muntjac deer (fawn) has a much loved image. They are used in cartoon films, books, greetings cards and to advertise commercial products. They have wide appeal.

The illustrations above show examples of the Muntjac and Fallow fawn. Both deer have spots when young, but mostly lose these as they grow to adults. Like many small, baby animals they tend to have large ears and eyes, with fluffy or fine hair.

In late Spring each year fawns are born. They are sometimes found by people who then think, because the mother is missing, that the youngster is an orphan. This is almost always a mistake. Mum will know where her baby is. If a fawn is handled by humans it will be deserted by the parents. Young animals, consequently, end up unnecessarily in nature centres, zoos, or being brought up by carers. If you stumble across a fawn, leave well alone — assuming it isn't obviously in distress.

Try your hand at drawing a Bambi picture. Begin with a basic construction then, as before, pop in the fine details with your gentle, controlled hand.

There is nothing hard about adding dot stipple, it just takes a bit of time.

Monarch of the Glen
The majestic Red deer stag has been a prized trophy for huntsmen throughout our history. It is still hunted today. You have, no doubt, seen stag heads in stately homes and halls, in museums and as a background prop on TV and in films.

Their superb antlers seem to serve no useful purpose other than as a status symbol. Stags head-butt other males when fighting occurs during the mating season, although they do not use their antlers as weapons. Nevertheless, don't go near a stag around May or October. You could be charged simply because you have invaded his territory.

41

The quality and maturity of a Red deer stag is usually determined by counting the number of points he has on his antlers. Twelve points indicate a fully grown male, which is known as a Royal. A fine beast may have more than 12 points.

Stags and hinds (females) are found on Exmoor, in the South West, the Lake District and the Scottish Highlands. In addition they are now farmed in many places.

Assignments

1. Draw from memory the basic shapes of a Fallow, a Muntjac and a Roe deer.
2. Draw from a trophy or photograph the head of a Fallow buck or a Red deer stag.
3. Draw a Bambi as a possible greetings card design.

Wild Red deer are very wary and soon put to flight, but those in captivity (like the one pictured above) are easily tamed. Notice the ruff of long hair round the stag's neck. The antlers have many points growing from a main branch. See how form and shape are suggested by dot stipple. Copy this example.

Horses are another ever-popular subject for artists and the general public. We shall work on a few of the scores of different kinds of horse. The much used and abused horse was one of the first wild animals to be tamed and domesticated by man. It has been used for a very wide range of jobs: ploughing, pulling heavy loads, carrying knights in armour and transporting whole armies. Without the mighty Shire horse it is doubtful whether, prior to the advent of the internal combustion engine, we could have fed our population growth as we did. Many elderly people still recall seeing these wonderful animals working in the fields and hauling heavy loads through our towns.

Horses have been used by man for centuries for riding, hunting, racing, performing and so on.

The hardest part first
In my opinion, the most difficult part of a horse to draw is the head because the skull is quite complex. It has many small bumps, hollows, ridges and curves. A head from the side is wedge shaped.

Study the way I have suggested bone under skin by using very fine dot stipple. Horses have big eyes, heavy upper eyelids, with long lashes. Their cheeks are prominent, and they have a bony ridge down to the nostrils which are surrounded by soft skin. Copy this illustration.

The head from the front is rather like the shape of a coffin. Try to memorise these shapes because then you will be able to draw a horse head from memory. Copy the illustration below.

 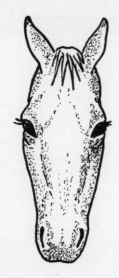

The whole lot

You may be an accomplished horseman or horsewoman and know far more than I about the anatomy of a horse, in which case you should have few problems in drawing a whole animal. We always draw well the things we know best. This is why artists need to know how things are put together.

I have had just one riding lesson in my life. A young horse called Rocket was allocated to me. While bouncing painfully along I imagined myself as a famous film star galloping through the Valley of Death. Later, after I had dismounted the frisky beast, someone commented that I was an awful rider. There is all too often a spoilsport around. My horse power has a wheel at each corner nowadays!

My sketch of a horse above will give you an idea of the general build of the animal. It will also demonstrate how dot stipple is used to show muscle, form and body shape. It is a most useful, yet simple, technique. Draw this example by starting with an accurate basic construction, then add the details. Be sure to position the eye in the correct place, and note how hooves, tail and mane are suggested.

A gentle giant

My favourite horse is the gentle giant called a Shire. This immensely powerful animal is one of the largest in the world. Its ancestors were the Medieval Great Horses which were bred in the Midland Shire, hence its name. For all its size and strength it is a friendly, easily managed animal which ought to be making a welcome return to farms, transport concerns and brewers' yards.

Have a look at the sketches on the right. Observe the sturdy legs, large feet mantled by long hair called feathers, the strong neck, shoulders and massive hind legs. A Shire horse can pull a load of five tonnes with no trouble. Copy this drawing in the usual way.

Wild ponies

The wild ponies on Dartmoor are accustomed to people. Thousands of tourists stop to admire, feed and photograph them. The ponies are small, tough, trustworthy animals who generally like children.

Above is a Dartmoor pony. Copy this by first drawing out the basic shape.

This is my drawing of an Exmoor pony. It is rare compared to the Dartmoor pony. In the Winter the Exmoor pony grows a thick coat of hair. When the Summer comes it moults to a thinner coat. Work out the basic shape, then draw this one in pencil or pen.

Draw an action horse

It was not until the camera was invented that the action of a running animal became evident to us. For centuries artists had tended to sketch and paint running animals with their front legs out and the hind legs stretched back in a similar way. Pictures of Victorian hunt scenes, for instance, depict horse, hound and fox all in this strange position.

I have illustrated just three of the many different positions for the legs of a running horse, above. Study these before copying them. Finish off with dot stipple, and a bit of background.

On the right is some close-up action. This was drawn from a photograph. Notice the way movement can be depicted by the horse's flying mane and the way the jockey is crouched forward with one hand on the reins, whilst the other clutches a whip. There is a suggestion of a brush fence with bits of it dislodged as the horse jumps over it. Draw your own version of my drawing.

Assignments

1. From a newspaper photograph draw a racehorse. Put in a suggestion of the background.

2. From life, or a good picture, draw a working Shire horse. Include in your picture a background to depict a farm or similar environment.

3. Draw a wild pony as a possible design for a birthday card. Think about a suitable background and then draw it.

CHAPTER 7
DOWN ON THE FARM

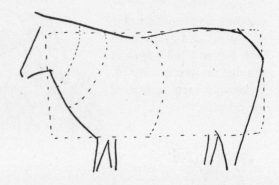

Counting sheep

I am going to show you how easy it will be for you to draw sheep. You may have noticed, when out of town, how many sheep there are. Thousands and thousands of them graze in meadows, fields, up mountains — almost everywhere. They are all pretty much alike in body shape — only their faces differ. There are white-faced sheep such as the Cheviot, Welsh mountain, Southdown and Romney breeds, while species of black-faced sheep include the Suffolk, Blackface, Yorkshire and Shropshire varieties.

Oblong with rounded ends

The basic shape of a sheep reminds me of an oblong with rounded ends, added to which are a thin leg at each corner, and a small wedge-shaped head. Once you get this image fixed in your mind you will *always* know how to set about drawing the animal.

The *detailed* shape of an animal can be suggested by the way fur, hair or markings are drawn. The body and limbs are rounded, like our own bits and pieces, so it would be wrong to use straight lines to depict hair or fur. Beginners tend to do just this, and then wonder why their animal appears to be flat sided. It is a help to pencil in lightly half-ovals as a guide.

Pay particular attention to the way I have drawn the wool coat. This was done with small wavy dashes running over the body contours and also down or along the outline of the coat — just the way it grows on the real creature. A few tiny dots on the face and legs denote skin texture. You will find that the humble dot and dash are most useful aids. You will be using this device often. You should find the illustration above quite easy to copy.

Above is a Suffolk ewe. Study the construction lines which fit into an imaginary box. Note how I have suggested ridges of thick wool. It isn't necessary to cover the whole animal with these markings. Indeed, doing that could make the drawing rather boring. All sheep have cleft hooves. Copy this example using my methods. I'm sure that you will achieve a super likeness and raise your own game as a budding artist within a matter of a few moments.

You must have noticed that sheep spend most of their waking time eating. The sketches above were drawn to show you how they look when feeding their little faces. Notice how the body curves have been suggested. When seen from a distance the eyes of a black-eyed sheep are not visible. Grass is suggested by short criss-cross strokes. Copy these examples.

Remember to *construct* every one of your drawings from a basic complete outline inwards. This is vital in all work. Many artists try to draw what they see a line at a time, in isolation from the whole. This is a big mistake because one wrong line — perhaps too long or too short — will cause all lines that follow to be wrong. Avoid this trap.

Lamb without mint sauce

Lambs, you will be pleased to learn, are far easier to draw than children! Little lambs have long legs, undeveloped coats and rounded heads. It is amazing how a beautiful little lamb quickly grows into a cumbersome, over-weight adult. After mature sheep are sheared they become, once more, leggy animals.

Notice how the rounded bodies of little lambs are suggested in the sketches above. Draw your own versions of these.

Get close

A good animal portrait makes an attractive picture. I have chosen the handsome ram's (tup's) head used as an emblem by Yorkshire National Park for the next sketch.

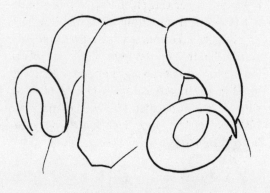

See how the construction lines must be accurate before details are added. Your problem here is to draw the horns correctly. In many rams the two horns do not match each other. My example shows this. Sketch, in pencil, the wedge-shaped face before putting in the curly horns. Start as in the upper illustration, then add the outlines of where the dark patches are to go; finally, pencil in the nostrils, mouth and eye.

Now look at the finished sketch below to see how all the shading is done. The optical illusion of round horn is obtained by using curved lines to suggest the form. Put in a few battle scars over and around the curved lines. The dark patches of hair are best created by making scores of tiny lines which follow the direction they grow on the animal. You will need to look carefully in order to get this right. Pop in a few lines in the white areas. Draw the long body hair as straggly streamers which point downwards. Sketch in the eye. Cast a critical look over your drawing then start to ink it in. This advanced picture will take a little time. I feel sure that you will manage it. Make space on your sideboard for your little gem!

It is not wise to approach a ram closely. They are very powerful animals. I was once charged by a young ram, but escaped injury by leaping onto the top of a large bale of straw! Take no chances: observe them, as I do, from behind a wall, fence, hedge or in a cattle market.

Go for it

I once came across a group of pretty creatures called Jacob's sheep. These are an ancient breed which are now gaining popularity. The lambs had black blotches against pure white. The adults had patches of dark brown. I sketched the original for the illustration below after watching them for half an hour.

I want you to copy this scene by working out for yourself the different basic shapes of the animals. Once you have done this correctly, in pencil, the drawing is quite straightforward. Pay particular attention to the curved back of one lamb, the stocky legs, shoulder blades, and rounded head. The standing lamb is nibbling the ear of its twin. Mother, in the background, keeps her eye on them. You will use lots of dots and dashes as shown in my drawing. When your pencil sketch is complete, draw over it with a size 0.1 pen. This is an ambitious picture but there is nothing in it which you can't do. Go for it!

Cattle
One of the most common beasts around our countryside is the cow. I see more black and white British Friesians than other breeds. The Friesian is a docile animal. Cows are usually curious about what humans are up to. They will stand still and look at you.

If you want to draw a bull from life do not take chances. They can sometimes be temperamental.

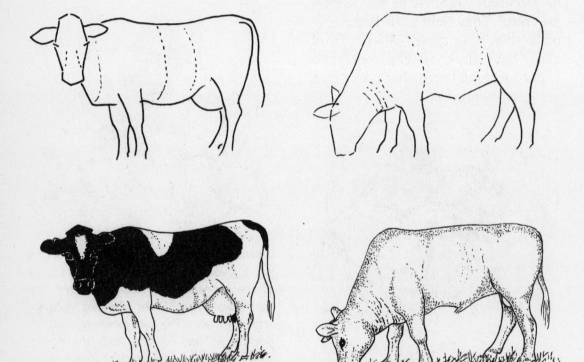

The sketch above is of a cow who found it fascinating that I should stop to draw her. See how the basic outline defines the sagging belly, slightly curved spine, coffin-like head shape, large ears, sturdy legs and deep chest. Try to fix in your mind the distinctive form. I use a small paintbrush and black ink to fill in the markings.

The animal I drew for the sketch above seemed to be gentle and unconcerned about me, but I worked from behind a wire fence just in case he wasn't! He was a huge beast with a cream coat, very short horns and strong shoulder muscles. See how dot stipple has been used to depict the power of the bull. Draw your version of him.

Giddy goats

Did you know that there are wild goats in certain parts of England? No? Nor did I until I became a rambler and discovered wild, or feral, goats in Snowdonia. They were nimble enough to leap from rocky hill ledges into the tops of trees in order to chomp leaves for their lunch. If I had not seen this spectacular event happen I would not have thought that it was possible. Wild goats can also be found on stretches of the Somerset coast. They tend to be larger animals than the tame variety. Feral goats have dark, shaggy coats and wicked looking horns that could give you a nasty prod!

Porky pigs

There are pig farms all over the place, so seeing pigs is quite easy (before the poor things become bacon, that is). I like watching these intelligent creatures. They seem to be forever hungry and constantly searching for food, over which they tussle noisily. The pig is quite cute and comical, so is much used by cartoonists.

All goats have oblong eye pupils. Copy these sketches of a friendly goat I met.

Notice the blunt snout, huge ears, small eyes, curly tail and small trotters. I used tiny dashes and dot stipple to depict the unusual skin. Draw a serious or funny sketch of a pig.

53

Cluck cluck

The striking design on the feathers of the cock bird (top sketch) consists of wavy, dark grey marks on a white background, which are particularly suited to pen work. See the odd way the tail feathers grow. The cock has a fine, impressive comb and large wattles hanging down below the sharp beak. Before you start to copy this bird have a look at the way I have drawn the basic form of a hen. The dotted lines help to give an illustration of the roundness in the bulky body. Sketch the construction lines before putting in all the time-consuming detailed markings.

Birds which we commonly see are dealt with in detail in the next Chapter, but you may care to start on birds by looking at the exotic farm fowl.

While it is nice to see an increase in free range chickens, most of these brown, stubby birds are kept for the number of eggs laid, and are not as attractive as the fancy fowl which I like to draw. I visited a nature centre to sketch the fowl for this chapter. Rare birds such as these are making a come-back from the old days of chicken keeping and showing.

There are many more friends on the farm, such as geese, turkeys, mules, donkeys, calves and others which I have not been able to cover in this chapter due to the problem of having too many subjects but not enough pages! There are none, however, that you cannot draw with great skill, following the methods you have learned so far.

Assignments

1.   Without looking back in this book, draw a lamb. Check your result.
2.   Carry out the same exercise with a Friesian cow and a pig.
3.   Draw chickens from life or photographs. Add in background details.

Having worked through this book your observation and drawing will be good enough for you to tackle bird art. Depicting our feathered friends requires keen vision, attention to detail, a good memory and ability with pen or pencil. That means you, doesn't it?

Many beginner artists think that birds are much too difficult to sketch because they rarely stay still for long, so they never attempt this fascinating subject. I once thought the same way, but became hooked on identifying the birds around me. I read many books and guides on birds, became increasingly interested in them and then began my art by copying photographs, drawings and specimens in museums. You can begin by copying my ink illustrations. Try using a 2B pencil to make things easier. My complete drawings here in this Chapter have close ink shading, but you can use very fine pencil lines and then smudge them with your finger to produce a wide range of lovely grey tones.

Head, beaks and bodies

Bird watchers are sometimes called 'twitchers'. A good twitcher can identify a bird in seconds. How is it done? It is a bit like aircraft recognition. The watcher learns about body, head, wing shape and a lot more,

including habitat, colour, flying characteristics, feeding habits and song or call.

The illustrations above show the head and beak differences between just four kinds of bird. The top four drawings are of a peregrine falcon. Under this is a duck, then a seagull and at the bottom a member of the finch family. Notice how the beak shapes differ. Copy these examples in pencil. Start by drawing the basic shape.

Most artists tend to draw birds in profile because they are easier to identify from this angle.

When I want to draw a bird I first take a good look at the overall shape of it. I then jot this down before adding beak, eye and wing details. It is a construction job.

Certain birds which can be seen feeding along seashores are called waders. One handsome fellow, a redshank, was the subject for the sketch below. Notice how simple these fast impressions have been kept. See how a bird can stretch or contract its neck, and the way it uses its long legs. Try to extend your skill by studying these illustrations for two minutes then jotting down what you saw. This is excellent practice for drawing from life.

The illustrations above are examples of my construction method. Copy these and try to sketch them quickly. With a little practice you will soon become good enough to draw some birds from memory, even after only a fleeting glimpse.

Recently, when watching birds on Derwentwater in the Lake District, I saw an angry male swan attack and kill a large duck. The poor duck was grabbed by its neck and held under water until it drowned.

Not content with murder, the swan swung the corpse round and round for five minutes. Swans are well known for defending their mate, young or nests, but in this case the swan seemed to be totally alone on the lake. These impressive birds all belong to the Queen. Maybe the one I watched will end up in the Tower of London!

Little dinosaurs

Birds are now thought to be the only living relatives of dinosaurs because they have a similar bone structure, lay eggs and make nests. Maybe it's just as well that the garden variety are small!

When swans are on guard they are rather like a battleship cruising into action. I drew one like this for the sketch above. I used a fine pen for putting in the feather detail. Always remember to leave a white spot in the upper eye. This keeps the swan awake! Draw your version of this swan.

These sketches show a sparrow at the top, a greenfinch in the middle and a chaffinch at the bottom. I have drawn wing and feather details to show you how they fit together, but it's not necessary to put in all these items. Notice how the three species seem to look alike, but a close study reveals slightly different wing, tail and beak formation. Start with a basic shape and then add the details.

Those of us who have a garden may frequently see a thrush or blackbird searching for a tasty worm or two. These two birds are alike in build but totally different in colouring. While writing this, I am able to watch a mother blackbird collect insects for her young which are in a nest close to my window. From time to time I rush out into the garden to scare off a marauding cat, magpie and/or the occasional squirrel. All are enemies of young garden birds.

There are many kinds of bird feet. Take a look at those below. The top left foot is that of a perching bird. These make up the majority of our feathered chums. The foot on the bottom left is that of a golden eagle. This has to be strong with sharp talons to hold and kill prey. The top right drawing shows the foot of a woodpecker. This has evolved so that this bird can grip on to bark tightly while it hunts for insects or hammers out a nesting hole. Woodpeckers don't give themselves nasty headaches because they have a brain which is suspended in liquid. You learn all sorts of things when you start out as a bird artist! The bottom right illustration is of a duck's webbed foot which, of course, is designed for paddling. Make notes of different feet.

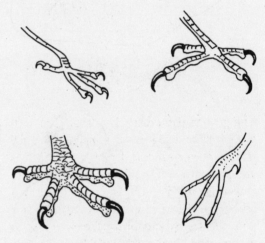

Copy the examples above.

It's nice for city dwellers to visit the sea in order to see exotic birds. I went to North Yorkshire to study and then sketch the birds for this Chapter. All these birds, plus hundreds more, were on the same crowded cliff face in the Royal Society for the Protection of Birds' reserve at Bempton.

58

Quackers
You need go no further than your local park pond, lake or stream to find your next subject.

The gannet, top sketch, is a large bird with a wing span equal to the height of a tall man. It makes spectacular high speed dives straight into the sea when fishing. The razor-bill, middle left (not to the same scale), hunts in a more sedate fashion. This is a darkly marked bird with white wing flashes. The little puffin, middle right, is a charming creature that is much persecuted by killer gulls and other predators. It has a large, multi-coloured bill for scooping up tiny sand eels. The gentle looking bird at the bottom is a kittiwake. This pretty creature spends most of its life on the wing so it was great to be able to see it at close quarters. Notice the black-tipped wing and tail feathers. Copy these fine birds at a larger scale.

The top illustration is of a mallard duck coming in to land, his tail fanned out as a 'brake'. The middle drawings are of a coot and a moorhen, which are often confused. The coot (middle left) is slightly larger than the moorhen (middle right) and their colourings are different. The tufted duck, bottom drawing, is black with white underneath. Draw your version of the pictures above.

Falcons

Falconry is now a popular sport. It is possible to see some magnificent birds of prey in reserves and zoos. Some garden centres now have the added attraction of a falconry which may contain a wide collection of birds of prey. There is one little falcon, however, which all who use England's motorways can see every few miles, although drivers mustn't allow themselves to be distracted from the road. The kestrel is the bird which hovers over motorway verges as it hunts for voles and insects. It is a very attractive creature.

Flighty

Experienced bird artists can recognise some birds by the way they fly. Study the flying shapes made by birds in your locality and before long you too will know your pigeon from your peregrine!

A male kestrel is pictured above. I sketched in each main feather shape before shading it in with close lines. Then the black markings were put in, with dot stipple used for the head feather markings. You can make a nice picture of this by using a soft pencil. Most bird pictures, by the way, are much better done as paintings, but before you can paint you need to learn how to draw your subjects accurately. Copy the kestrel.

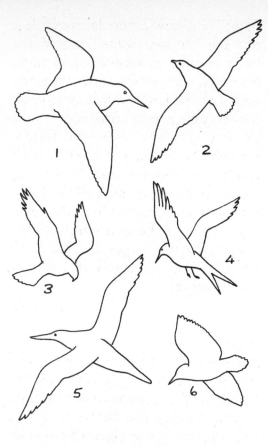

1.   Draw a garden bird from life.
2.   Observe a bird in flight and then jot down in your sketch pad your impression of it.
3.   From life or a photograph, draw a bird portrait.
4.   Sketch birds in their natural environment by drawing in suggestions of the background.

I have drawn six different birds in flight for the sketch above. Number I is an oyster catcher. This is a black and white bird which has a red beak. I'm surprised that it is called an oyster catcher because oysters only form a tiny proportion of its diet. 2 is a kittiwake; 3 a hovering kestrel; 4 a common tern (I once visited a nesting site of this highly active little bird — it was on a freezing cold wet day which gave me quite a turn!); number 5 is a sketch of a gannet scaled down to fit in here; and 6 is a woodpecker. Try sketching these interesting shapes.

CHAPTER 9
ODDS AND ENDS

Sometimes it is necessary to use photographs in order to draw certain subjects. Working from a photo does not mean copying it exactly. More often than not, photographs lack the composition or clarity which an artist may need. The aim should be, therefore, to use the information which a photograph can give. It is like a writer using a dictionary.

Scaling up or down
Before you begin to work from photographs I will explain how to scale up (enlarge) a drawing and how to sketch from a large picture. It's a very useful device to have handy and one that is used by commercial artists.

You will require a sheet or two of clear plastic of the sort used with overhead projectors. On this you mark a grid with the aid of a rule and a black pen. Start with a grid of 1cm squares. This is the one to lay over the photograph or drawing that you wish to work from. Your next task is to draw very lightly in pencil another grid onto your drawing paper. You can make this 2cm squares — if you want to double the size of the image in the photo. Then you simply transfer, square by square, what is in the photograph to your drawing paper.

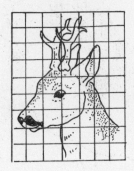

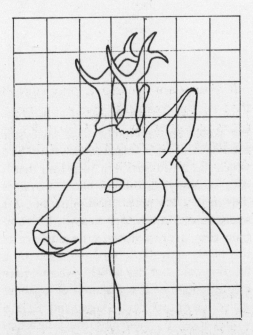

Above is my scaling up, to double size, a picture of a Roe deer. The top illustration shows the small grid, the lower sketch shows the basic lines drawn out in pencil on the larger grid. When satisfied with this operation I inked over the pencil lines and, when they were dry, erased out any which showed, together with the grid lines.

The last job was to finish off by putting in the details. Below is the complete drawing.

If you want to use a photograph that is, for example, twice or more times as big as you want your drawing to be, you would make a grid with 2, 3 or 4cm squares, depending on the measurements, to lay on it and then a pencil-made small grid of 1cm squares on your pad or paper. Now take time to make your own grid.

Shading

As you have worked through previous chapters you have learnt a little about shading by copying some of my drawings. I have found that the most used shading, in animal pictures, is a dot stipple of various densities.

Take a look at the shading examples below. I have used a pen size 0.5 and 0.1 to make these sketches. The finest dots are obtained by the way you use your pen. For this you use a gentle grip and just lightly dab the paper. For stronger dots you simply increase the pressure of your fingers or use a larger size of pen.

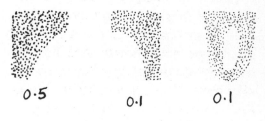

0.5   0.1   0.1

The shading in the examples below is close-line shading. This can be used vertically, diagonally, curved or whatever, in order to give the effect you want. Just remember to keep all the lines the same distance apart and, usually, running the same way. The darkest patches or shade are best done with cross-hatching, as in the middle drawing.

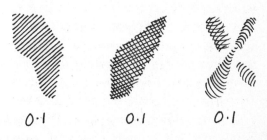

0.1   0.1   0.1

Great action drawings

Newspaper shots of subjects in action are great to use. I drew the racehorse on the right from a daily paper's sports page. The original showed a group of horses, but I selected just one to draw. Notice how a streaming tail and bits of flying turf help to convey action. You might try scaling this up twice the size when you draw your own version of it.

I enjoy sketching horses, so I turned my attention to another one for the sketch on the left. The newspaper depicted a dark horse jumping against a background of dark hedge. For my drawing I made the horse pale and subdued the hedge. I then put in a little shadow on the ground and over the hedge to show the horse better. Shadows are another useful device for artists. Scale up this picture for a bit more practice.

One of my favourite animals is the highly intelligent dolphin. This mammal (warm blooded) has always been man's great friend but, sadly, all humans do not return this friendliness. Some fishermen still hunt it, while others kill it in drift-netting used for tuna fishing. Other dolphins become performing prisoners in sideshows and marine parks. The dolphin must be a very forgiving animal!

The bottle-nose dolphin above, however, was photographed enjoying a natural life in the ocean. See how its jump is captured by a curved body, explosion of water and spray of drops, as the dolphin is about to plunge back into the sea. Note the way I have used shading to suggest waves and dot stipple for the skin texture. Scale up and draw your own version of this charming creature.

Animal portraits

When you consider drawing an animal portrait, keep in mind that you need to isolate the subject from a complicated background. Often, the best work is one that concentrates solely on the animal's head, expressive eyes and character. A portrait of a bird, however, is perhaps more attractive if the whole bird is drawn with, maybe, just a hint of its environment put in.

Several years ago I had a spot of beginner's luck when I photographed a tame eagle owl. My snapshot was good enough to draw, paint and sculpt from. I have used it again to draw another portrait of this magnificent bird of prey. It was a large specimen with golden eyes and a pale chest streaked with black and brown markings, some of which were rather like a herring bone in shape. The head, body and wings were mixed shades of mottled brown against a cream background.

An owl has four toes. It will sometimes perch with two toes forward and two back. The one illustrated had three toes forward on one foot and two showing on the other one.

If you ever handle an owl you will find that it feels just like the softest silk. This is because its feathers are particularly light and covered by a fine down on the underside. It has evolved this way to enable it to fly silently when hunting. A deaf wood mouse stands no chance against it!

The eagle owl is quite common in zoos, parks and some garden centres.

See if you can reproduce my drawing three times larger than the printed size. To do this would need a grid of 1cm squares on my sketch and 3cm squares in light pencil on your pad.

Pet portraits
Baby animals and domestic pets make good portraits and are very popular pictures. Become good at this skill and you can earn money with it. People will always pay for a good likeness of their favourite pet.

The grey wagtail, drawn above, is an attractive bird which is found near rivers, streams and lakes, where it feeds on water insects. It has a blue grey head and back, yellow chest with a black bib, black and white wings and tail, and white flashes above and below the eyes. I used dot stipple shading to suggest shadow on the rock and to fill in part of the bird. Reflections in the water have been depicted by short, wavy lines of different widths. Scale this drawing up to about twice the size of the printed one.

The lamb and young rabbit above are ideal for drawn portraits. Notice how shadow is used to pick out the face and bone structure beneath the fur. See how you get on by scaling them up for pencil studies. A larger size will enable you to put in more of the coat detail.

I could not resist drawing a portrait of a Basset Hound. This gentle, affectionate dog is a popular pet which has been made famous through films, television and strip cartoons in newspapers. Despite his rather sad-looking face this animal has great physical stamina, and an excellent nose which can be used to track deer, hares or rabbits.

Before moving on
It has not been possible to cover all animals in this section, but I hope that the ones you have practised drawing will encourage you to portray any creature on our planet!

Look at the sketch above. The wrinkled forehead, face and long, dropping, velvety ears help to give him a worried image. Take a note of how the coat has been drawn. The deep-set eyes have a patch of pink skin (haw) showing beneath the eye-ball. Carefully study all the details before drawing your version, first lightly in pencil then in ink.

CHAPTER 10
BEGINNING TO DRAW FLOWERS

Flower power

You, like me, must like flowers. Thousands of would-be flower artists begin by trying to paint flowers before learning how to draw them. This is the wrong route to go and the hardest. You are already well ahead and on the right road to becoming successful.

The ability to sketch flowers is easy to acquire if you go about it the right way. What is the right way? First of all you need to learn to look properly at your subject. By this I mean being able to see how many petals a flower has, what shape they are, what kind of leaves, how they are marked, what the stem is like and so on. After a little practice you will soon absorb all the information required to enable you to churn out masterpieces.

When you look down at a flower, what do you see? Almost all flowers seen from above are either round or oval. A huge number of flowers have five petals. So the shape and number of petals is the same for many species. You begin your drawing by first using a pencil to sketch a rough but accurate basic picture. This drawing, in fact, is the most important one. If it is more or less correct, refining it into a finished ink or pencil picture is easy. Remember to make your drawing larger than those reproduced in this book as big drawings are easier to draw.

Be dotty

The useful form of shading called dot stipple, which you have previously used for drawing animals' fur, will be used a lot in this section. You can practise being dotty by gently and quickly tapping your pen up and down on your art paper. Copy the patterns shown below, noticing how deep shadows are obtained just by increasing the number of dots in a particular area. This comes in handy when depicting dark shadows.

Flowing lines

I have noticed that a nervous pupil may have a spot of trouble making long, smooth lines such as those required to illustrate a flower stem. It's usually caused by lack of confidence, or inexperience at drawing.

I should like you to practise making long strokes in one unbroken, flowing movement, just as you may do when ironing something long. The best way I've found to produce long lines is to allow my right wrist to rest on the paper then, with pen firmly held, move my hand up, down, across or whichever way is needed. Look at the shapes below before trying this out for yourself. The time you spend on this will be well worthwhile.

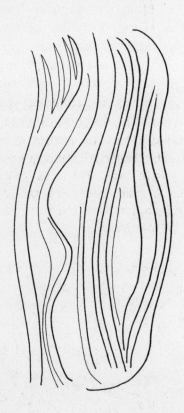

The snowdrops above were drawn from life. Notice how dot stipple has been used on the stem and also to suggest soil. Study the rough drawing below before attempting your version. Always remember that it is the early rough sketches which are the most important when constructing a flower picture. Knock off the rough edges to end up with an accurate pencil drawing of the bunch. The final operation is simply inking in the sketch then erasing out the pencil lines, leaving a good margin round your drawing.

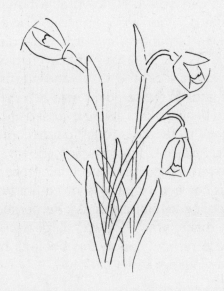

Early starters
Let's crack on now and get drawing some flowers. When the first snow-drops peep out I know that Spring is on the way, regardless of the fact that it might be blowing a blizzard or rain is coming down like stair-rods at the time. Let's start with these cheerful blooms.

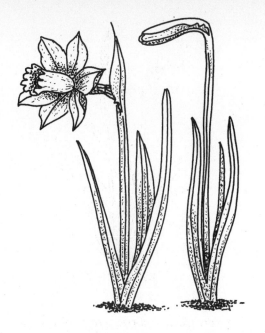

Above is my illustration of a miniature daffodil in full bloom with another flower about to pop out of a bud. See how the flower slips out of the stem. There are fine lines on the stem and leaves. Dot stipple is again used to depict shadow and soil. The sketch below should help you to draw this plant without difficulty.

The sketch above depicts another very early starter. It's called the *helleborus* but is commonly known as the Christmas Rose. This flower is a dull purple with dark purple veins. The area round the stamen is pale green. See the drawing below before tackling the fine pen work used on this plant.

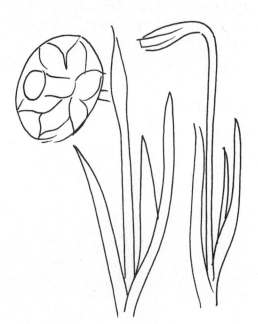

A seed factory

Each annual flower (those that grow from seed each year) is a superb seed factory. The diagram below reveals the inner structure of the plant. The central club-shaped bit is called a pistil. This is the female part of the blossom which is surrounded by the male parts called stamens. When the pollen grains are ripe they are discharged through the anther. Along comes a bee, insect, bird or puff of wind to scatter the grains. Some of the grains will eventually drop on the tacky stigma. Then they grow down into the pistil to fertilise the eggs (ovules) to become seeds. The cycle then starts all over again. Isn't nature wonderful?

One of my lovely pansies can be seen in the sketch above. This plant makes a superb ink drawing. Notice how dot stipple is used to depict a colour change. Study the rough sketch below before creating your own little gem.

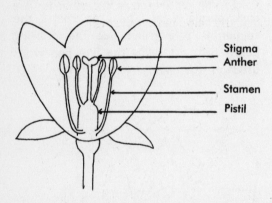

Stigma
Anther

Stamen

Pistil

Spring has sprung

You know when Spring has finally arrived by the position of the sun, the cheerful din made by birds and the kind of plants sprouting through the soil. I like to plant a few pansies in my garden. It's a delight to see them from the kitchen window, as their bright little faces follow the sun throughout the day. A bit like me!

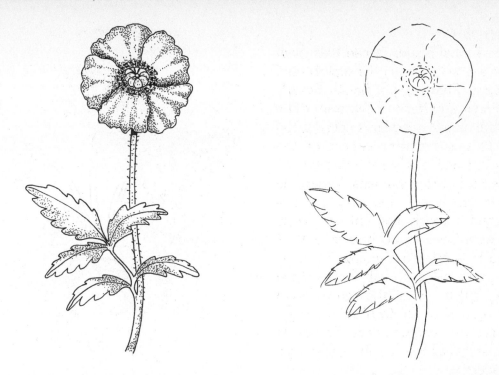

The common poppy is a super flower. In the sketch on the left you can clearly see the pistil surrounded by a double row of stamens. This flower makes a very good ink drawing. See how the dot stipple works effectively. Is your version going to be yet another eye-catcher for the sideboard? I'm sure you will manage after looking at the help lines on the right.

Tulips are other plants which are easy to care for. I plant the bulbs in containers or baskets and leave them be. They spout through the Spring. My bright red tulips appear in black and white for the illustrations to the left and right. Note the bell-shaped flowers with tightly packed petals. Draw a little work of art from these.

Merry month

May is usually a delightful month. It heralds the approach of high Summer, brings forth a wide range of flowers, gives us more sunshine and more daylight hours to work or play in. And brings on hay fever!

The sketch below shows asters. These flowers have many forms. I used the little, blue ones. They are an excellent border plant. You should find them very easy to draw.

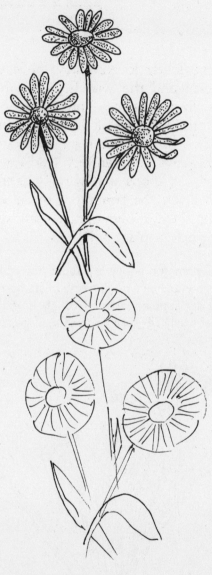

This striking new flower is the pink malope which derives from a Spanish wild flower. Notice how dot stipple is used to darken the shadows to show off the petals in my sketch. Now you try this trick!

Assignments

1. Draw from life any small flower.
2. Draw a plant with three flower heads.
3. Draw a perennial flower.
4. Make an ink drawing of a container of May flowers.

CHAPTER 11
A WILD BUNCH

Most flower lovers enjoy the countryside and the wild flowers which are found in it. This chapter is devoted to some of the lovely specimens which can be seen and drawn. Nowadays you can buy wild flower seeds in shops and garden centres and enjoy the beauty of these wild things in your own back garden, window box or plant pot!

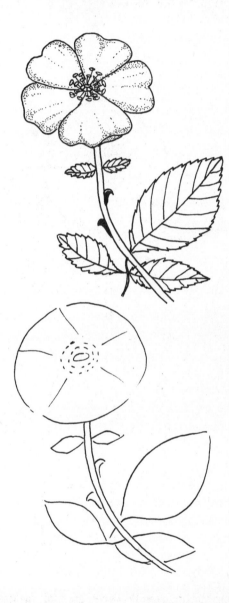

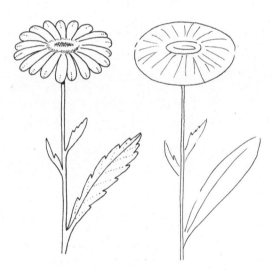

The ox-eye daisy is a common wild flower found in waste areas, on railway embankments and many other places. It is a tall perennial plant which has striking white petals with a yellow centre. The illustration above shows how simple this flower is to draw. You should sketch this one in under ten minutes and with one eye closed!

We all must have come across the wild dog rose in our countryside. It likes wild places, tall hedgerows and shrubs. The picture above should help you to sketch this flower.

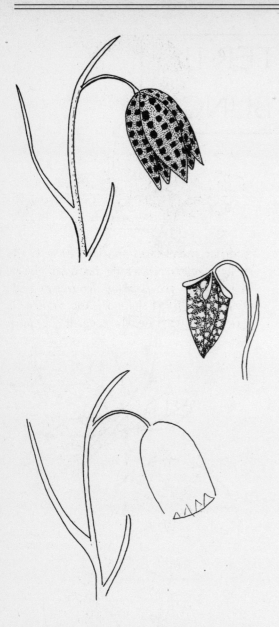

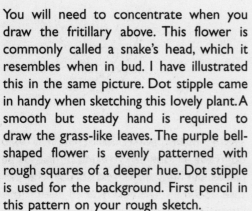

The columbine, above, is another striking wild flower. It has a bell-shaped flower which has petals draped round it. Each petal has a spur which curls upwards. Try your hand at working out the rough shape for yourself before copying this sketch. When you are done, it should be no trouble at all to do the same for the beautiful tree mallow below. Notice the white areas I have left on the petals where the light reflects from the shiny surfaces.

You will need to concentrate when you draw the fritillary above. This flower is commonly called a snake's head, which it resembles when in bud. I have illustrated this in the same picture. Dot stipple came in handy when sketching this lovely plant. A smooth but steady hand is required to draw the grass-like leaves. The purple bell-shaped flower is evenly patterned with rough squares of a deeper hue. Dot stipple is used for the background. First pencil in this pattern on your rough sketch.

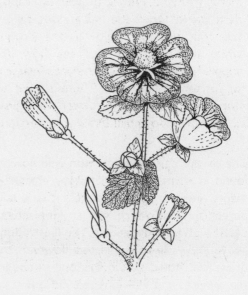

Romp in a swamp

There are enough wild plants in our countryside to fill several books. Some wild plants thrive in wet places, particularly swamps. When you visit the great outdoors take along your wellington boots in case you happen across a flower-strewn bog!

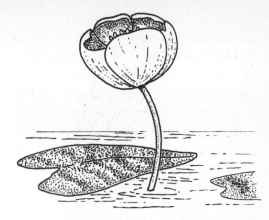

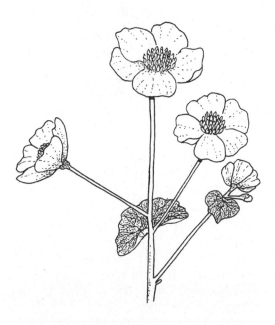

Another member of the lily family is the striking yellow water-lily featured above. This flower grows away from the pads which are heart-shaped. Dot stipple is again useful on the lily pads. Try a quick sketch of it.

Above is the beautiful yellow-flowered marsh marigold. Notice the kidney-shaped, dark leaves. Draw the basic shape before you copy this one. Below is the glowing white water lily. You will see how dot stipple has been used on the pads. Water is suggested by fine lines. These should be horizontal otherwise the water will appear to run up or downhill! Draw your version .

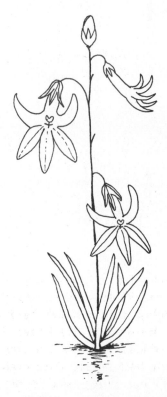

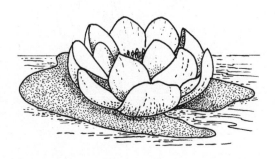

Above is the water lobelia which likes to grow in lakes which have acid water. It has pale lilac-coloured flowers. You should have no trouble copying this plant — drawing the basic shape first, of course!

On the rocks

In the nineteen-seventies there was a boom in rockeries and suitable plants for them. Many gardens still have a rockery filled with Alpine plants as the large rocks used for the job last forever.

Alpine flowers, though small, are very pretty. There are hundreds of attractive species which are well worth drawing — let's try your skill out on just a few of them.

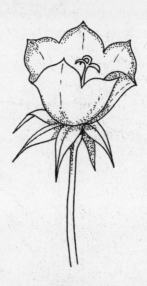

This bellflower makes an attractive little sketch. See how dot stipple is used on this flower. It is pale lilac with a yellow stamen. The bell shape should make it easier for you to establish the basic outline of this one, before you complete your finished drawing.

To the left is a rockery pink, which is round with the usual five petals which are pink with dark pink spots and dashes. Dot stipple once again proves handy to depict this.

Below is a sketch of snow-in-summer flowers which grow like mad. They are ideal for growing in walls, cracks in paving and for covering ground. You shouldn't have much trouble drawing your own version of these.

The illustration below shows a heron's bill Alpine plant. This flower is ground hugging.

Notice how I have treated the unusual leaves before you make your drawings.

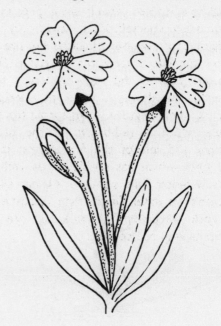

Bottom left you will see a group of soapwort flowers. These are tubular, flat-faced pink flowers. Bottom right is a mountain buttercup. This little flower is a beautiful golden yellow.

This illustration should improve your drawing skills but don't try to do it without taking a break. After sketching half or less of the picture, take a breather. Clean the oven, dust the attic or have a quick nap before finishing your own masterpiece.

The illustration above will give you a good challenge. It's not difficult but it does take time. Allow yourself one to two hours for this one. To make the job easier, be sure to draw the layout accurately as above. The flowers topping the rock are called fire dragon. This flower is red with a yellow centre. The dull green leaves sprout from a stem which is red-brown at the base. Below and left of the fire dragon is a ramonda which has purple petals with a yellow centre. This is another Alpine which doesn't like water. On the right, opposite, is a rock cinquefoil. This one has orange blooms with red centres.

Assignments
1. Accurately draw a dandelion from life.
2. From life or a photograph, draw a flower which can be found by the sea.
3. Try visiting a garden centre to sketch from life another Alpine plant.
4. From life, accurately draw a rock, pebbles and a plant.

CHAPTER 12
AN ENGLISH COUNTRY GARDEN

Smelling of roses

Amongst my students, the rose is one of the most popular flowers to draw. There are hundreds of different species, some old and many new. A rose can be flat, cupped, pointed, rounded, rosette, pompon or urn–shaped. They are particularly popular in English gardens — both in town and country!

Because there are so many varieties of rose, it is vital that you look carefully at your subject before starting to draw it.

Above is the bright red Alexander rose, which is one of the many large-flowered bush roses. The orange-pink Royal Dane below is another. Notice how dot stipple is used to depict small folds and creases on the petals of the Alexander, whereas tiny fine lines were used on the Royal Dane. Make good drawings of these two and add them to your masterpiece collection.

This big, beautiful, yellow rose is called Grandpa Dickson — I wonder who he was?! This flower is easy to draw. Grandpa Dickson, by the way, is around 18cm across. Perhaps he was a big chap? Look well, then draw your version.

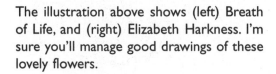

The illustration above shows (left) Breath of Life, and (right) Elizabeth Harkness. I'm sure you'll manage good drawings of these lovely flowers.

The bright red miniature rose illustrated on the left, above, is called Sheri Anne. Next to Sheri is a salmon-pink large-flowered bush job named Silver Jubilee. Your drawings will take quite a time so take a little break halfway through.

Yet another large-flowered bush rose is Just Joey, above. What a wonderful name! Take note of how the petal edges are serrated and uneven. The many small, fine creases in petals should be depicted with fine lines. Putting them in requires a very light touch.

The Incense Rose (above left) is a small shrub rose which is cupped with primrose-yellow petals. It has yellow stamen. The small leaves are greyish-green. The bush rose on the right side of the picture above is a rose of similar colour named Canary Bird. Draw these little ones carefully.

Climbing up the wall

Climbing plants are very popular with most gardeners. They are used to cover walls, fences, sheds and out-houses. Like a lot of folk I have them over my fences and to hide grotty walls.

If you have worked your way through this book you should have reached a very good standard of draughtsmanship. You won't have any problems sketching climbers.

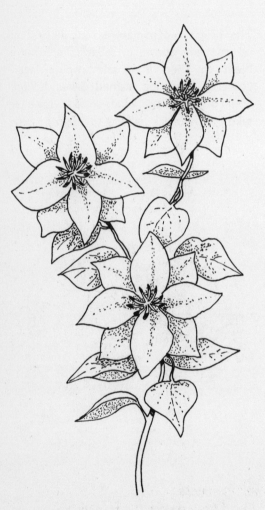

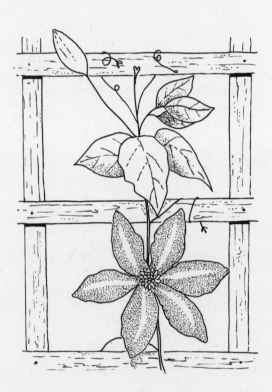

The clematis above is pink-white with yellow stamen. It's an easy flower for you to draw. You will, of course, notice how dot stipple is popped in to highlight some petals.

I am unable to tell you what this lovely clematis above is called. The label blew away months ago! It has beautiful, big, lilac and purple flowers. The purple bit runs down the centre of each petal. The leaves are a fresh green. Snails love them. When you make your version of this sketch, notice the way wood grain has been suggested in the trellis supporting the plant.

The climber drawn below is caled Nelly Moser. She's a very big girl, beautifully turned out in white and pink. The pink parts are shown by stipple. As ever, lay out the basic shape before you ink in a superb copy of this one.

The unfortunate-sounding Black-eyed Susan makes a lovely drawing, and an even better painting. Susan has orange petals with a black-eye in the centre. Dot stipple was useful to help pick out the five-petalled flowers.

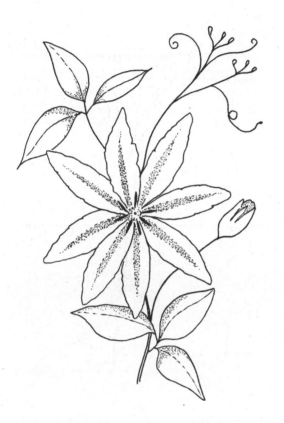
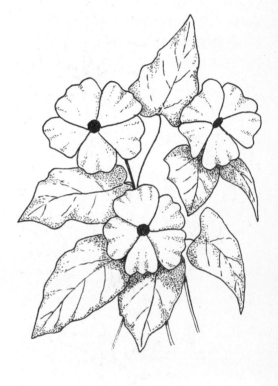

Reminders

Are you remembering to leave a nice wide border round your master-pieces? Are you making your draw-ings larger than the printed versions? You do, of course, erase pencil marks from finished sketches? You do? Good — no smacked hands for you, then!

Assignments

1. Draw a rose bush from life.
2. Choose a climbing rose to draw.
3. Draw a climber used to cover a wall.

CHAPTER 13
GO POTTY

If you do not have a garden, pot plants provide the means to enrich your environment, improve the atmosphere and act as good models for you to draw.

Design your own greetings cards
If you can draw some of the flowers in this chapter accurately, you might consider turning them into your own personal greetings cards. Perhaps you have access to a PC and scanner, and so could make multiple copies?

This drawing of a cyclamen uses hundreds of tiny dots to shade in the leaves. It will help you to pencil in lightly the white veins on each leaf before using a dot stipple. See how the same technique has been used to shade in the pot. Notice also how by increasing the dots in some areas you can suggest deeper shadows. Have a go!

The Busy Lizzie is a popular indoor flower. The one drawn above was white. When making your own gem, notice that dot stipple is mostly used for leaves, shadows and the pot.

The trick of using shade to highlight leaves and flowers can be seen in the begonia drawing, below. The flower illustrated was a pale orange which was a deeper colour in the centre of the petals. Quite beautiful. See if you can capture some of this beauty in your depiction.

The pink geranium sketched above should be easy for you to draw. Notice the dark rings on each leaf, depicted by dot stipple. There were many more flowers on my plant but I thinned it down a bit. This plant's pot is rather attractive. It has a rough surface contained between smooth top and bottom flanges. See how shading has been used for this. Your version of this sketch might make a nice postcard-size personal card. Reduced in size, you could use it on your letterheaded stationery.

85

Barrels, bins and buckets
Container gardening is another popular branch of the garden scene. Plants will grow in almost anything. My friends and I have used all manner of items in which to house flowers. I have seen ex-waste bins, old barrels, mop buckets, wash basins and ancient bath tubs, all awash with beautiful flowers.

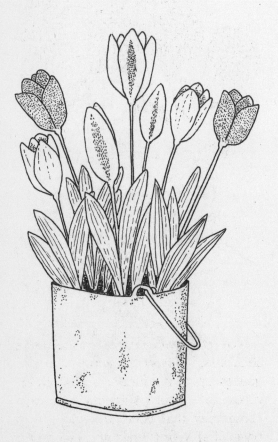

Don't throw your old buckets away. They make excellent containers for all sorts of flowers. Above is a bucket full of mixed tulips. Three are yellow with a vivid red flash, two are bright red, with the remaining two yellow.

A small, wooden barrel features in the sketch above. This is interesting to draw — you could, if you wish, fill it with the flowers of your choice. I used gazania, which are small, orange-yellow daisy-like flowers with silver leaves. There are three mixed lilies sprouting up from the silver foliage. Notice how the tub has been shaded. Now begin your own masterpiece.

Mixed petunias are wonderful flowers to cram into bins, buckets or the attractive terracotta containers sold in most garden centres. I used a friend's to draw the sketch below. The multi-colours of the plants would make a nice bright painting, as an alternative to this attractive black and white picture.

You should have no trouble with drawing your version of the sketch below. The zinnias were yellow-orange, the leaves a dark green.

Plastic fantastic
Modern plastic replicas of old cooking pots make good containers for small plants which can be grown from bulbs or seeds. I used to have several of these plastic pots, but now there is only one due to my golf practice. Does this mean that my swing is improving?

Now that you have finished this section on flower drawing, you are geared up to produce wonderful pictures of your subjects. Always remember that *good drawing* is the basis of all worthwhile art. I've found that the effort you put into drawing is rewarded a hundredfold. Try not to have long spells without doing any sketching. Practice really does lead to near perfection!

CHAPTER 14
EASY LANDSCAPES

I love wild places and mountain scenes in particular. Originally I took up mountain walking to overcome my nervousness of heights. This condition was cured in three days. Now, I enjoy a great sense of satisfaction and achievement when I stand on the summit of a mountain.

Personally, I have found that rambling and sketching combine well. There is no doubt that weekend rambling is an ever increasing popular activity which has particular appeal for artistic and 'green' people.

Below is a scene viewed from up on the Cuillin central ridge on the island of Skye, in Scotland. I discovered this panorama during what was, for me, the hardest and most exciting of mountain walks yet undertaken. By the way, always walk with a friend, or a group. Mountains can be dangerous, as well as beautiful.

Special equipment?

By now you should have the most important equipment necessary to beginning work as a landscape artist — a good selection of pens and pencils, a supply of paper and, most important of all, bags of confidence!

When you sit at a table in your kitchen-cum-studio, or wherever you decide to produce your masterpieces, a drawing board is also useful. A purpose-made artists' board is expensive, but strong plywood or chipboard is fine. I use a 50cm by 50cm piece of chipboard both for drawing and watercolour painting. One end I prop up to give a sloping surface, which helps the eye and makes drawing easier. Two hefty books do the job.

Some of the pictures in this section were drawn later, from photographs. On a hard walk, or in difficult, windy weather, a camera is therefore useful.

Generally, though, the outlay on gear for landscape drawing is much lower than for other art mediums. The satisfaction you will receive from this hobby will be worth many times more than any money spent. When your pictures reach an advanced standard you could well sell one, and recover all your costs. Isn't that a happy, encouraging thought?

An easy start

All the drawings you do from this book should be bigger than the printed version. A larger drawing is usually easier to work on anyway. Use an A4 pad or typing paper for the following exercises.

Fill in the white paper

Illustrators and artists need to know how to fill a blank sheet of paper. This is done both with the lines of the drawing and with shading. The latter marks are used to suggest different forms, distance and so on. You have already used several forms of shading in your previous work in this book. Use the most simple of shading for your first few landscape exercises.

Begin with the very simple illustration below. This is called an extended landscape because it covers a large area of land. I happened upon this scene while on a ramble, and took a photograph of it from the vantage point of a hill top. Draw this lightly in pencil. Leave a border round your work. This is a good habit to get into as it will give your sketches a professional look. You will probably find it helps if you start by drawing the outline rectangle inside which you wish to keep. Try working from top to bottom, as I do; it helps if you follow a methodical procedure.

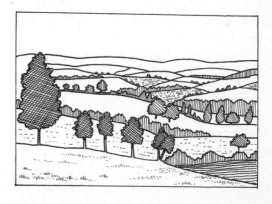

Above is the same sketch, filled in and developed. Notice how distant patches of forest, hedges and trees are recorded by vertical, even-spaced fine lines; how the field in the foreground is drawn with horizontal shading. Meadows further away are suggested by broken lines and small dashes. Trees in the foreground are made to look darker by cross-hatching. Grass is shown as little lines, dots and dashes. Go over your pencil copy of this drawing, then rub out the pencil marks. Isn't it easy? You could do this with one eye closed!

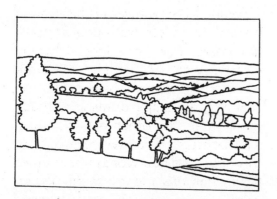

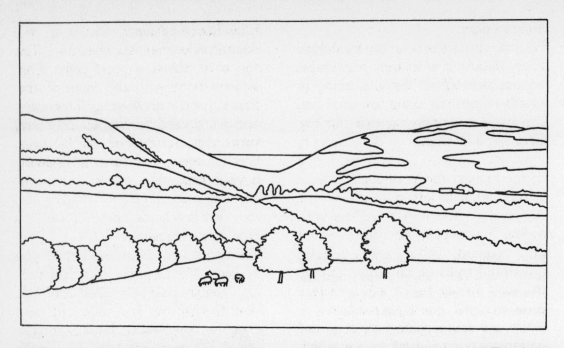

Above is a scene on the Isle of Wight. Take a long, careful *look* then draw in pencil. The sheep depicted in the middle distance look like small oblongs with rounded ends. No detail is visible from a distance.

Below is a simple, shaded in version of the same sketch. The trees to the left are partly cross-hatched, to create a feeling of depth. The middle ones are fully cross-hatched, which brings the trees forward, towards the eye. Try it.

Simplification

Beginner artists tend to try to include every details of what they see. This is impossible! Who has the time to spend a month drawing one tree? You can leave exact copying to a camera. What you must aim to do is simplify what you want to draw. Indeed, one of the highest forms of art is that in which detail is left out, the artists suggesting what things are like with as few lines as possible. You have a lot of freedom. You can remove unwanted trees or buildings, change the way a river runs, or put in features that will improve a picture.

You are learning step-by-step the quickest way to reach a very high level of skill. Don't try too hard to produce identical copies of my drawings. That is not important at this stage. I want you to develop your own style. You can use your own ideas about how to create shading. We are all different, and express ourselves in our own, unique way. One of my aims is to teach you basic drawing and shading, so that when you unleash yourself on, for example, the highlands of Scotland, you will know how to draw any scene that captures your attention. It would be very frustrating to sit before a breathtaking scene, pen poised over pad, and not know what to do!

Look for pictures as you go about your daily toil. Think how things could be simplified. We often take for granted those scenes with which we live constantly. When you take your spouse, children, or dog for a walk, look around for pictures. If you glide off to work in your chauffeured Rolls-Royce, take a squint at the countryside you are passing. The top of a bus is a good place from which to scan your environment. Parks, pretty gardens, golf courses, and all kinds of other local beauty spots will provide possible pictures. Part of being an artist is knowing how to *look*.

Practice makes perfect

The more you draw, the better you become. We all know that, but success requires self-discipline too! We tend to take the easy way out (and expect to succeed without putting in the drawing hours) but this works against us when learning a skill like drawing. It's interesting to know, however, that when newcomers begin to show good results, their drawing tends quickly to become pleasantly addictive. I hope this will soon apply to you. Keep a small sketch pad with you and force yourself to draw scenes within easy reach. If you can't get about, use photographs, old Christmas or greetings cards, and so on.

Another step forward

So far, all the landscapes I have suggested you draw have been very simple, and probably not worth framing. Very soon, however, you will make progress. Your first masterpiece is not far away!

On the right is an outline sketch, drawn from a road-side in Scotland. Draw this either straight off with a pen, or lightly in pencil first.

On the left is the same sketch, shaded and completed. Notice how thin, close lines are used to break up the white area of the sky. Leaves are suggested on the near trees, then lightly shaded over by diagonal lines. A few extra lines denote clefts in the rock in the foreground. The lines used for grass are more detailed near the artist, but they fade into dots and dashes further away. Now finish your picture in a similar fashion.

Aim to create an eye-catching gem, which will hang on your kitchen wall. It will become the talking point for all visitors. You know the sort of thing: "I did this from the top of Snowdon. We went there to exercise my bad leg but I couldn't resist dashing off a quickie of the wonderful scene below me!"

Shading, with a little practice, should be done rapidly. To go fast is better. It helps to cut down errors because there isn't time to worry about, or doubt, your ability. Just be bold and confident. Ignore minor mistakes; indeed, expect them and take them in your stride.

This illustration on the right is the most advanced one in this section. It has been drawn in stages, as shown below. Making a landscape drawing is a construction job.

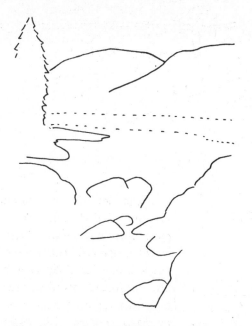

Stage one of copying this drawing is shown above. Use a size 0.5 pen to draw the mountains, near the river bank, and the large rocks. Notice how much blank paper there is to fill as you define your outlines.

Stage two, on the left, shows how a little more major detail is added. Now you have a few ripples to indicate water, broken outlines of trees in the foothills and more detail in the boulders and the single fir tree. Put the changes in with the same pen.

Return to the illustration above to complete the sketch. Change to your 0.1 pen. Draw the sky first, then the distant trees and the shading on the hills. Now shade the middle banks and the boulders. Fine cracks on the rocks and the small wavy lines in the water are the last for you to tackle. You have now finished your most advanced picture. Congratulations! You are on your way!

CHAPTER 15
DON'T RUSH YOUR BRIDGES

Loiter with intent

Bridges are a common feature of the British countryside, and they are often used by artists as the centre-piece of a landscape picture. I shall show you how to obtain the effect of rock and stone, and give you an idea of how a bridge is constructed.

Whenever you come across a nice looking bridge, don't rush across it! Walk around, under and over the bridge. Try to fathom how the builders put it together. Did they use local materials? Is it an ancient structure? Who uses it? Would it make a good picture?

This different structure is a fairly new bridge in Scotland. Natural rock was used for the buttresses of the bridge and perfectly cut rectangle stones for the sides. Copy this sketch. Draw the straight lines in pencil with a ruler. Small dots and dashes suggest the texture of rock.

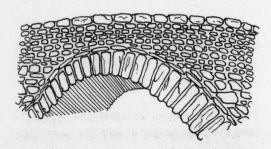

This is a bridge in the Yorkshire Dales. Large slabs of local stone were used for the central arch. Stone and rocks, set in mortar, form the sides and are topped by big ridge stones. Each stone has been separately drawn. It's easy to draw. Have a shot at it.

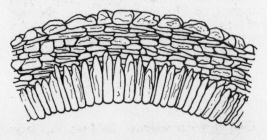

This is an ancient pack-horse bridge. See how tightly each rock fits into the whole design? No mortar was used, rather like dry stone walling in construction. A size 0.1 pen was used for all these bridge drawings. Now you try them, drawing each stone and rock separately.

By now you will know that ink illustrations take time and patience rather than a great talent. Artists find time to improve their crafts. I am sure you will do the same now you have joined our ranks.

A tip worth remembering, when drawing walls, bridges and some buildings is that it isn't necessary to copy each individual rock or stone exactly. This would take ages to do. Although each piece will need to be drawn individually, the best way is to decide what shapes the material has, and then draw *similar* shapes.

Your first little gem

I have used Wantendlath bridge for the sketch above. This old pack-horse bridge straddles a stream which comes from a tarn at the foot of impressive hills. Wantendlath is a hamlet of small cottages and farm buildings which nestle between steep rocky mountains. I drew the structure with no background detail.

One very hot summer day I sat on a large boulder to draw a picture. A pony took interest in the event. He was feeling peckish, and raided my bag for sandwiches, as you can see above! Fortunately there was a tea shop handy so all was not lost!

Look at the sketch above, then copy this in pencil. When you are satisfied with your outlines, complete the drawing with a size 0.1 pen to match my completed illustration. See how stones, grass and water have been suggested. There is nothing too difficult for you to manage.

The sketch above of the same bridge was taken from the opposite side. Below is the basic pencil drawing. First, put in the sky lines with a 0.1 pen. Add the distant hill line and then the main bridge construction. Draw stone shapes one-by-one, leaving two small gaps on the bridge for where tufts of grass have grown. Put in the five bar gate. Flesh out, almost black, the fir trees.

Shade in the rock, the underside of the bridge and add the clumps of grass. Lightly shade some of the stones on the bridge with diagonal lines. Portray water by wavy horizontal lines. Finally, jot down some more grass by short, spiky strokes. Now ink a frame round your drawing and choose a space on the wall!

I have used dot stipple on the stone work on the bridge on the right. The heavy stones are simply wedged together without mortar. Dot stipple suggests their form. It can also be used for depicting trees and many other subjects. Take a challenge! Copy this straight off with your 0.1 size pen.

As a small reward for your efforts, copy the landscape with bridge in the illustration above. Shading is mostly by vertical and diagonal lines and by cross-hatching. Dots, dashes and tiny oblongs record the bridge material. Radiating, broken lines give an effect of space in the sky. You should have no trouble with this one.

Assignments
1. Study as many different types of bridge as you can, making notes of the different shapes and brick work.
2. Practise drawing rough stone with dot stipple.

CHAPTER 16
TANGLE WITH TIMBER

Get to know trees

The more you know about the subjects that you want to draw, the easier it is for you to refine the detail. As you can guess, it boils down to having a good *look* first. So far you have drawn trees in a simple way. Now I shall show you how to depict trees with added realism. In many landscape pictures trees tend to be in the middle or far distance. They can be handled on the simple lines learned hitherto. However, where a tree is the main foreground subject in an illustration, in order to draw it accurately you need to know how to obtain the detailed effects of bark, branches and foliage.

What problems must you solve? First ask yourself what shape the tree is. Is it round, tall, or spread out? What do the leaves look like? Are they fine, broad, pointed or odd shaped? What is the bark like? Smooth, craggy, ridged, ringed or what? As with all subjects, it is essential constantly to re-examine the construction of the items that go into a picture.

The drawings on the right illustrate how to depict foliage, trunk and branches. Notice how dark shadows help to give the trees depth and form. The top drawing, a maple tree, has been shaded on one side and almost blocked out where the deep shadows are.

A few small, fine pen strokes were used to suggest the grain of the bark. The two trees in the middle were shaded after they were drawn, with light, short strokes. These were cross-hatched to give deep shadows. The bottom sketches were deliberately enlarged to show you how to make your foliage. Copy these trees in pencil, then go over with a size 0.1 pen.

Control your scribble

Winter trees

The effect of leaves and shadows to make up the sort of tree drawn above is created by what I call controlled scribble. *After* the main tree shape has been drawn with fine, dotted pencil lines (later to be erased), this outline is filled by controlled scribble. Hold your pen fairly loosely. Make quick, small twirls, circles, squiggles, wiggles, dots and dashes. Produce deep, dark shadows with white bits showing through to give a sense of texture and form. It's easy with practice. Now try your own scribble!

After the leaves have fallen in Winter, we can see clearly how a tree is constructed, and how one differs from another. Look at the elm at the top of the illustration above. See how different it is from the poplar, birch and fir below it?

Patience and good observation are required to draw a Winter tree accurately. Once again you must ask yourself exactly what it is you see. What shape is the tree or bush? Which way do its branches grow — up, out or down? What are the twigs like? How does the bark appear — ridged, wrinkled or smooth?

The best way to start your drawing of a winter tree is with an outline shape. I then move to the trunk, follow by putting in main branches and, last of all, add the twigs. The only problem with this kind of picture is that it takes time, but any attractive drawing is well worth a small slice of our precious life. Besides, it keeps us off the streets!

You don't have to use the identical shapes or shading which I have used. You may prefer to express your own ideas of how to obtain similar results. You could easily become the best tree artist in the whole world. I hope that you do!

Trees to the front
Artists frequently use trees as a focal point in a picture.

The sketch above shows how a group of fir trees on an island has been used in the foreground to give an idea of the scale of the mountains beyond. Copy this drawing. Start with the sky lines to suggest cloud movement there, then sketch in the hills, followed by the island and the tall trees. The bank of middle-distance trees is portrayed with a controlled scribble. The same technique is applied to the bushes on the island. The fir branches are suggested by masses of two, three or four short strokes drawn with a fine pen. Notice how some of these point upwards, while others go downwards. The portrayal of water is obtained by wavy, horizontal dashes as in previous work. This little picture could be another one for your kitchen wall!

How is your bark?

For a good tree to be featured as the main subject of a picture you must know how to produce realistic looking bark.

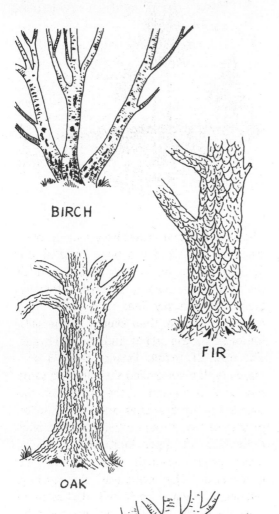

BIRCH

FIR

OAK

BEECH

The sketch on the left, drawn in one of my local parks, shows four types of bark. The beautiful silver birch tree is a popular subject for landscape work, and is simple to draw. See how the white trunk is marred by triangular black blotches which increase in number towards the base of the tree. The bark surface pattern is shown by curved lines which run around the trunk. The branches are dark in tone and this is shown by shading.

The trunk of a fir tree is quite different. The bark is made up of large overlapping scales which appear to hang down the tree. Each of these slate-like pieces, when viewed close up, can be seen to have small flakes in its make-up. I have depicted them with a few lines.

The common oak, often drawn or painted by artists, is nice to sketch. The bark is composed of rough, deep ridges, with many cracks and crannies. These trees have heavy, sometimes twisted, branches.

The beech tree is another common tree which is fine to draw. The bark lines go around the trunk and are smooth compared to those of the oak.

See how the roots are suggested on the different trees. Copy all the drawings straight off with a size 0.1 pen.

A point to remember, with trees, is to draw one side in shadow, with markings more detailed than the opposite side. This helps to create depth and shape. If you use the same way of depicting bark for the whole trunk, it will look flat. Make one side lighter, with less detail.

Go behind the bushes
It pays to spend a bit of time behind the bushes, in the name of art of course!

Assignments
1. Draw your nearest tree.
2. Draw the trunks of four different trees.
3. Look at some bushes and then draw them with a controlled scribble.
4. Examine the foliage of a tree in the distance. Then draw the tree.

The sketches above show how bushes and small shrubs are drawn. Notice how the scribbled, dense shadows tend to project the lighter parts and this helps to suggest the form of a bush. Trunks and branches are only partly seen. Copy these examples for more practice scribbling.

CHAPTER 17
TAKE TO THE HILLS

You should have gained some skill in sketching rocks and stone in Chapter 15. Your experience will now be extended. I will show you how to draw the huge boulders and rocks which feature in many mountain scenes.

The island of Skye, for me, has the most wonderful mountain range in the UK. The Lake District and the Scottish Highlands come a close second. I will, however, for this chapter take you, via sketches, mainly on a visit to one of the majestic peaks of the Black Cuillin mountains of Skye. My drawings began on a visit when I once clambered up there on a hot summer day.

Rocks and boulders simply drawn

Above is a sketch of some boulders, drawn very simply. Fine lines suggest cracks, splits and texture.

This sketch is of rock slabs with small ridges and cracks. Heavy infilling is used for the darkest parts.

These are all easy drawing jobs. Copy them all before moving on.

The above illustration is of a cairn, which is a heap of stones used to way-mark mountain walks. Notice the vertical lines and the cross-hatching used to depict shadow.

Now try sketching the illustration below. The new technique here is one for shading clouds. They are best outlined lightly in pencil; then you use a pen to put in the sky lines round the fluffy shapes; finally you erase the pencil outlines. Go on to shade your mountain. Use cross-hatching to make deep shadow. The rocks in the foreground show well in contrast to the mountains beyond.

The sketch on the right takes you a step further on. It has a similar cloud and sky effect, but the mountains contain slightly more shading than those in previous sketches. Lots of little lines were used in a kind of controlled scribble. The sea is suggested by horizontal lines. The reflection of the lowest hill, nearest the sea, is depicted by wavy lines. Copy this picture.

The illustration below has dark-looking mountains which are easy to draw. The dense areas were obtained with cross-hatching. After sketching this example in ink, you could draw it again in pencil or using coloured crayon. It is useful to increase the range of your artistic skill. Each medium brings a different majesty to the picture. Try them and see!

Interesting rock structures

On the Island of Skye I came across a beautiful bay. The rock formation in the bay, shown above, was fascinating. The rock structure was buff-coloured, and it had several kinds of texture. There were slabs, boulders, splits and pebble size projections.

The sketch below is of the basic shape of this ancient natural architecture. Draw the outline in pencil then proceed in ink, as above. I started with the sky lines, then moved on to the dot stipple on the high point of the rock. I worked slowly down to the deep shadow under the shelf, and then suggested with fine lines the lava layers.

A trip to the top

The remaining drawings in this Chapter illustrate my trip to the top of Sgurr Alasdair, which is a naked rock pinnacle on the central ridge of the Cuillin mountains on Skye. I was a novice hill-walker then but had the good fortune to be escorted by a superb leader who prompted me to try to become a good all-round rambler. If you ever attempt this walk be sure to allow the best part of a day for it. The going is hard and mostly uphill over varied terrain.

Awe-inspiring peaks

This sketch shows part of the region along the way. The distant peaks were the object of my journey. The ground was littered with huge slabs between which tough clumps of red grass grew. I used a size 0.1 pen to draw this. Draw your version of it. If you decide to scale it up to a much larger size than in this book then use a size 0.5 pen.

To give you an idea of the immense size of its awe-inspiring peaks portrayed above I have put two figures in. Be prepared to spend two hours or more on this picture. Start with a pencil drawing. Examine the drawing and work out how I have done the shading as part of your study of how to portray mountainous terrain. If your attention does flag, stop for a break, then resume your masterpiece for the lounge wall.

Off to the seaside
You may, like me, enjoy a spot of beachcombing or a romp along wind-swept shores. After all your practice on landscapes, you already have the ability to draw a good seascape! The techniques for your pen are essentially the same.

An attractive seashore may, at first glance, seem to contain very little. Below is an example. There are two jagged rocks, a line of distant cliffs and a few gulls. Breakers with ever decreasing waves lap over wet sand which reflects the rock shapes. There is a pale sun which sets off an unusual pattern of clouds.

Drawing this picture was quite easy. I began with a line for the horizon and then put in the rocks. I gave these substance by using plenty of cross-hatching but I was careful to leave the rock edges bare. This was to show where sunlight was reflected. Waves and breakers I formed by using different thicknesses of line. I made extensive use of wavy lines, dashes and dots and created seaweed with a controlled scribble. Look carefully at the gulls. Note the rough oval shape of the body with a neck that can stretch or contract. The beak is short and slightly curved at the tip. The eyes are set fairly high in the head. I used light shading to distinguish the grey wings and the back of the birds in the sun. See where the light and dark areas are. But note the different treatment of the birds in the shadow of the rock. Now copy this illustration with a size 0.1 pen.

The huge rock below is in Guernsey and was the subject of a painting by Renoir. For an ink drawing it becomes a useful study of dark and light. I employed dense cross-hatching on the deeply shadowed side of the rock, vertical lines to shade the jagged headland in the distance and small dashes for ripples on the sea. A few patches of seaweed and three gulls were easy to add in order to complete this simple scene. I produced this drawing to a small scale with a size 0.1 pen. It will help if you can make yours twice as big.

I drew the human in the above sketch quite simply. Figures of this kind are often used to add a little interest to pictures. They don't need much detail. I included the girl to give an impression of freedom and space. Notice the way she walks into the scene rather than out of it. This is an important composition point. You want your viewer to look into and around your masterpieces, so design them with this in mind. I will return to this aspect later on. If you have no experience at figure drawing try a few quick pencil sketches before you start with pen work. Then have a go at this illustration.

The scene above is a little more ambitious, but just as straightforward to draw. It shows one of the many natural mini-harbours on Guernsey. I have put in two small wader birds in the foreground and a contemplative figure at the edge of the sea. The diagonal sky lines suggest space and wind movement. The boat is not slap bang in the middle of the picture. As you will discover in Chapter 19, placing it dead-centre would show bad composition. The object of attention is best put to one side so that the drawing is not divided into equal halves. Simple when you know how, isn't it? Copy this example or a similar one.

Quiz

1. What is the best way to fill in deep shadow?
2. What would you use dot stipple for?
3. Fine lines are good for what?
4. Which lines are best used to depict the sea?

Answers

1. Cross-hatching or heavy infilling.
2. Stone, trees, bushes, rocks and many other subjects.
3. Fine details of all kinds.
4. Short, wavy ones, sometimes of different thicknesses.

CHAPTER 18
BUILDINGS IN LANDSCAPES

Self-discipline

Different artists have different pet subjects. It could be that you don't have much enthusiasm for drawing buildings, but it is important to be self-disciplined in order to become skilled. It pays to tackle all subjects in a professional way. The skill required, for example, to draw buildings accurately is just the same as that needed for drawing trees, animals, people, or whatever. All problems of draughtsmanship are related. It is only the way we think about them that varies.

I have had students who, at first, shunned drawing a certain subject, only to find out after trying that what was feared proved to be that at which they were best! Learn to draw *everything* well. Then you can specialise . . .

Start with basic construction lines

You are about to learn how to draw some of the buildings which crop up in landscapes. At this point in the book I won't worry you with the rules of perspective. There will be more about them in the next Chapter. Obtaining the correct angle of slope in a roof, or the slanting lines of a building, is mostly a matter of good observation to experienced artists. You will learn to apply such experience as you progress.

Copy this illustration of an old barn by first putting down all the main construction lines, as shown. Position this book and your piece of paper beside each other. With the book held flat by in one hand, lay your pencil or pen lengthwise along the main ridge of the roof with the other hand. Transfer the pen's angle to your piece of paper. Do the same for the other angled lines and slopes to gain information about perspective. I used dot stipple to denote texture in the large rocks. The ivy-covered tree was added for interest.

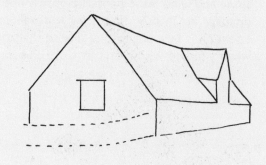

Drawing sloping lines from life correctly is very nearly as easy. Simply hold up your pen or pencil between you and the line you are after, match the angle, then transfer that line down onto your masterpiece.

Variety is good

There are many types of building scattered around the British countryside. The ones that are totally different from modern dwellings are often the most interesting for us to sketch. Windmills, for instance, are not normally found next to the supermarket in the High Street! Flat country such as Holland, or the English Fens, is a better place to look for them.

Draw the old church above and note how one side of the building has been shaded. The humble dot and dash are wonderful devices for artists. Here, they achieve the impression of stone with ease.

Old ruins are simple to draw and quite interesting to see. The heap of rocks sketched below is all that remains of a castle in the Yorkshire Dales. Sheep follow everywhere; I put in two to give a sense of scale. A copy of this example should take about half an hour. Off you go!

The illustration above shows the way a windmill can dominate land it stands on. This particular specimen is both round and tapered. Draw the outlines in pencil first. Make sure your basic lines are right before completing it in ink.

Farm buildings

Modern farms with water towers, stock sheds and massive barns are not always very pleasant to see. There are, however, still a few traditional farms about.

The sketch above shows farm buildings set against a background of hills. Dot stipple seemed the obvious way to suggest the large areas of scree (loose stones). Draw this example; it could be another little gem for your hall, along with the sheep shelter and bridge shown below. The latter drawing is a good example of dot stipple work.

In the above sketch of a farm in the Yorkshire Dales I did not include a pile of rocks and an unsightly shed. My original sketch was only 13cm across. I used a size 0.1 pen. The dry stone wall in the foreground was made up of many different sized stones of various shades. The wooden gate just about hung together and it tilted at an angle to the wall. The house was small with white-painted walls. There were tall clumps of reddish grass sprouting from the swampy ground and, of course, the 'inevitable' sheep. The distant hills and patchwork of fields gave a sense of space and freedom. Copy this illustration.

In Wales and Scotland you sometimes come across a stone built cottage of the sort illustrated above. I expect these picturesque dwellings are hard to live in if you are used to the creature-comforts of a town house. They are, however, a delightful feature for the landscape artist. A cottage set against a background of impressive hills, like the one above, should by now be straightforward for you to copy.

Quiz	*Answers*
1. What is your first task in drawing a landscape?	1. Take a long, good *look*.
2. How should you start?	2. With a basic outline sketch.
3. What is the main problem in drawing buildings?	3. Getting the slopes right (perspective).
4. Which drawing techniques are useful for them?	4. Dots and dashes, controlled scribble, fine lines and shading.

Be a good composer

If you have not already done so, you may now feel confident enough to tackle drawing from photographs. To be successful you also need to know how to compose a good picture. A camera records things as they are, rather than as an artist wants them to be. Most of us become snap-happy when we are on holiday. What looks perfectly lovely through a view-finder often turns out tiny and distant in the resulting snapshot. Somehow it can seem only half the scene you expected. Photographs can nevertheless provide excellent information for a drawing.

As an artist you are free to alter any scene you choose to draw. Two of the greatest English painters changed what they saw in order to produce great works of art. They were John Constable and JMW Turner. I recall visiting a waterfall in the Yorkshire Dales, specially to see where one magnificent masterpiece had been painted. The painting concerned was done with sparkling golds, yellows and the brilliant use of white and colour to create hazy water-splash mist. What I found when I got to the force (waterfall) was a let-down. The water trickled over a black rock ledge, only to splash down onto more dark rocks. Perhaps the weather had been too dry for too long

— but then, I cannot claim Turner's vision or superb technique.

Common mistakes

Beginner artists tend to ignore composition both through lack of knowledge and the struggle to put down accurate lines. Composition in art refers to the arrangement of things. The most common mistake is to put the horizon far too high up in a drawing. Eye-level in any picture must fall on the imaginary line which lies directly ahead of you when you draw that scene. As you can see from the illustration below, you cannot start drawing a landscape seated and then stand up half-way through! Eye-level must remain constant.

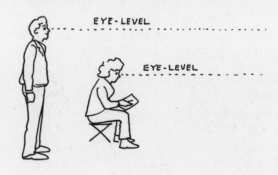

A low horizon will give an impression of great space and calm. To test how different eye-levels affect pictures, look at whatever scene is in front of you now. Stand on a chair to

look; then sit down and, finally, lie down to look. The latter position is one sometimes used by photographers and artists to give an unusual viewpoint. The ideal level for the horizon is usually about a third of the way up from the bottom edge of the drawing.

The sketches below show correct and incorrect eye-levels and another aspect of composition.

Another common error is shown below.

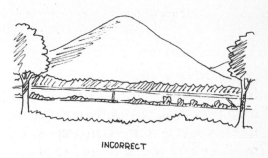

The sketch above has a series of horizontal lines, two opposing trees and a hill in the centre.

The two trees in the sketch above are both the same shape and size and are equidistant from you. They therefore divide attention.

This drawing demonstrates improvements that you can make. Shift the hill off centre, move the trees and rearrange the fields so that the eye is led into the scene. No earth-moving equipment required for these renovations!

In the correct version above I have balanced one tree against three, placed at different distances. You now see the house as the object of attention.

115

When learning how to draw landscapes you are tempted to concentrate solely on the items which make up your picture, and to forget about the composition.

Use your freedom

INCORRECT

INCORRECT

The incorrect sketch above has two hills, two trees and two boats which appear to be heading out of the scene. The high horizon does not help this faulty composition. Curiously, odd numbers — 1, 3, 5, etc. — are an aid to composition.

The faulty composition above doesn't seem too bad at first glance, but look how much better the correct version below is. A raised river bank now prevents the river running out of the picture. A large tree on the right balances the small groups on the left. Eye-level has been brought down to give a greater impression of distance. Just a little thought given before *beginning* a drawing can make a huge difference to the finished job.

CORRECT

CORRECT

In this correct drawing, three boats sail into the picture. Two different size trees are balanced by a broken, rugged shore-line. A lower horizon flattens down the hills and a distant headland has been added.

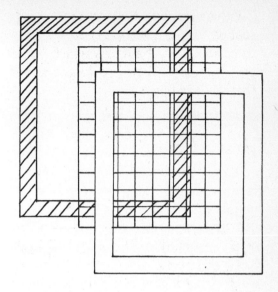

Be uninhibited about changing what you see into what you want to portray. Feel free to chop out, pop in, shift, curve, bend, straighten or whatever. Remember, you are an artist, not a camera.

There are exceptions to taking such liberties. For example, you might be commissioned by your millionaire aunt or uncle to draw the ancestral home accurately. Then you would show every cracked windowpane, broken roof tile, dent in the ramparts, and patch of rising damp — or would you?

You can glean a great deal about excellence in composition by visiting a good art gallery and studying the work of old masters. The trick, once you have absorbed what you will — having stood in front of a particular masterpiece — is to remember what your eye *saw first* and then how you looked around the rest of the painting. Next, have a good think. What had the artist done to make your eye move the way it did? What you discover will give you ideas for your own creations.

A bad composition is one which people won't waste time looking at. Perhaps it is too confusing to the eye; maybe no single item grabs the attention; possibly there are too many conflicting objects.

A useful little aid
A grid is a handy aid for artists of all abilities. It is easy to make out of a transparent sheet, marked in squares and sandwiched between two cardboard frames.

Many famous people in the world of art have used grids. Vincent Van Gogh, for instance, made quite a large one on a stand. He mentioned the gadget in letters to his long-suffering brother who sponsored him throughout his life. Van Gogh used a grid to make a painting of his bed in the asylum at Arles. This picture, which was sold for millions of pounds, is a good example of accurate perspective drawing. Vincent, like me, was a self-taught artist. The comparison ends there — I've no intention of lopping off an ear or shooting myself!

Long before Van Gogh was born, artists made grids and used them to study perspective. This artists' tool has been around for a very long time.

How to make a grid
The grid I use was made in half-an-hour from two pieces of scrap cardboard, a sheet of transparent material of the kind used for overhead projectors, and a little glue.

The screen is divided into 2cm squares, perhaps eight up and eight across. You can use different measurements or sizes to suit yourself.

Your first job is to mark out squares, in ink, on the transparent sheet. Use a rule or straight edge, and a sharp blade to cut out two identical cardboard frames. These frames should have their external measurements slightly larger than the grid and their internal ones somewhat smaller than the grid. Lay one frame down on a flat surface and put a few dabs of glue along the borders. Carefully position the transparent sheet down onto the cardboard. Prepare the other frame with glue and then lower it down onto the grid so that the two frames stick together. A heavy book on top will hold everything in place until the glue dries. That's all there is to making a very useful drawing aid!

gutter line in relation to the horizontal in your picture.

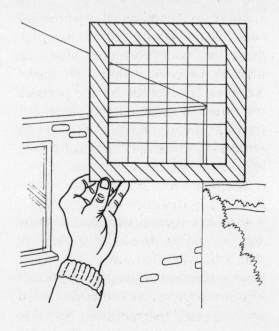

How to use a grid

A grid can be used inside or outside on most subjects. I hold mine at arms' length in my left hand so that, while I am taking frequent squints through it at the object in view, my right hand is free to draw. You can, for example, hold your grid half way to your face in order to view a larger scene. This works well but you must remember for any particular picture always to hold it at the same distance from your eyes and to line it up exactly on the same place each time. For example, on a wall that you can fairly assume the builder built vertical! Then you can see at once what angle to draw, say, the

From my simple example above you should be able to appreciate how you will also now be able to use a grid to capture accuracy in lines of perspective to a degree you may never have imagined possible before. The same tool can be used in a slightly modified way as an aid to drawing still-life subjects: trees, hills, humans and no end of other things. First, pencil lightly onto your paper or pad the *same number* of squares you have on your grid. You can then make accurate sketches simply by matching what you draw onto your pad squares to what you see in your grid squares.

If you have read the previous sections in this book, you will remember from page 62 that a grid can be used to scale a portrait up or down. Provided the number of squares in the grid you place over a portrait is the *same* as the number of squares on your pad it doesn't matter whether those on your pad are larger or smaller; the point is that if an object occupies 2.5 squares on the portrait grid, then it must fill the same 2.5 squares on your pad grid. If you keep everything in its rightful square then your copy will be a true one. If you wanted to you could enlarge the drawings in this book using a grid.

A grid is particularly useful when drawing village scenes from life. A glance through the screen will reveal exactly where the lines of the buildings converge, as their distance from you increases (perspective). You can use it to see just how the edges of a road merge, perhaps round a curve and out of sight, into the distance. It

may help you to suggest the camber of a road accurately.

Help with landscapes
Beginner artists faced with a vast spectacular panorama which covers scores of miles often try to cram the lot onto a small A5 sketch pad! This is a common mistake which use of a grid will prevent. The picture to be drawn in the sketch on the left, for example, is that part in the frame.

If you want to draw a wide landscape, and there's no reason why you shouldn't, you could still use a grid, but it would have to be wide enough to cover the scene. This entails making a much bigger screen. I personally don't thinks it's worth carting around more than one small grid. Frequent use of this will teach you quickly what to look for, and what to draw. You will gain the experience to tackle panoramic scenes with suitably huge confidence and enthusiasm without the need for a giant grid.

Perspective without fear
As I have tried to show you, perspective can be learned naturally by discovering how to look. Experience leads to knowing whether a sketch is right or wrong. A grid is a great aid too. Now, however, I shall explain the theory of perspective. With practice, all should become clear.

Perspective applies to all things seen and drawn. However, beginners still tend to be confused. Perhaps the dreaded word itself puts them into shock! Nonetheless, it remains common for budding artists not to know quite how to handle perspective.

A vanishing point

Imagine that you are standing on a hill. You look across a perfectly flat plain which is divided by perfectly square tree-lined fields. The sketch below shows this unlikely scene.

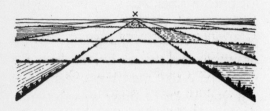

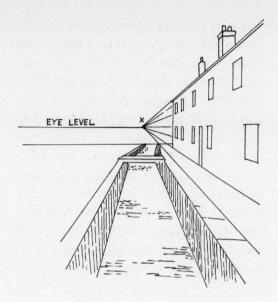

Your eye-level is the distant horizontal line. The spot at which *all* 'going away' dividing lines converge is called the vanishing point. I have marked this with a cross. You can see what happens to these lines and how this affects the crossing lines. Although we know these are square fields, they are not drawn square; to make the picture look correct they each have to diminish towards your eye-level. This is a very basic way of understanding perspective. That wasn't so bad, was it?

We usually become aware of perspective when we start to draw a building. The sketch at the top right of this page shows how perspective applies to a row of houses which are to the right of the viewer. I have simplified this drawing of a village named Darlington, which is in Northamptonshire, so that you can concentrate on the perspective. I stood on a footbridge so that the buildings were to my right, and my eye-level and the vanishing point (X) were straight ahead.

See how the straight lines, if extended from the window ledges, roofs, chimneys, pavements, and stream before it takes a curve to the right, would all converge at the vanishing point. The bend in the stream beyond the bridge means that its lines do not follow the others all the way.

The sketch below shows what happens when one or more buildings are different from those they adjoin. It is possible to have more than one vanishing point in the same picture. Note that a vanishing point can itself vanish! It can be off your picture to either side.

If putting your drawings in perspective is causing you problems, the answer for you (as for all!) is simple. First put in your eye-level. Then remember that all perspective lines run to there. The sketch below illustrates how two rows of trees here (they could be a row of houses) have *two* vanishing points along the same eye-level. It doesn't matter that the trees in either row may be different heights or shapes, the vanishing point stays the same for all the trees in each row.

When you sit and draw, your eye-level remains constant. It follows then that all the vanishing points you need will always be *on this same line*. Newcomers go wrong here — their eye-level moves about. In reality this only happens if you hop up and down!

Don't let perspective bother you. In most general landscape drawing you will manage fine with pen, pencil, grid and your own good eyes. If you like sketching buildings, and many do, then what you have just read will help you to produce correct work.

Quiz
1. What is good composition?
2. Why is your eye-level important?
3. Why use a grid?
4. What is a vanishing point?

Answers
1. An arrangement that is easy to look at.
2. Your eye-level should determine where your horizon is.
3. It will improve your drawing.
4. A spot on the eye-level where lines converge.

CHAPTER 20
OUT AND ABOUT

Down in the village

Your grid will be useful for copying drawings in this chapter. We're going down to the village to see what stirs. Ancient hamlets and villages are part of England's rich heritage. They are attractive features of our land, and have particular appeal for many city dwellers. Each village has its own character and architecture.

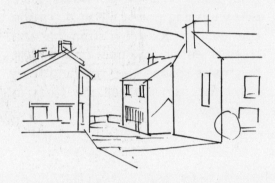

The village of Dent in the Yorkshire Dales is a clean, charming example, depicted in the sketch above. These cottages are over-looked by high fells. The roofs are made of hand-cut rock slabs which are very heavy. Those at the bottom of the roof are larger than the ones at the top. In the left foreground bright red tulips were in contrast with smart yellow specimens in the back rows.

My ink illustration was produced on a small pad with a size 0.1 pen. I kept the scene as simple as possible. I preferred shading to denote strong shadow, rather than blocking in too heavily. Study the basic construction lines above before starting your own copy. Get these right and the result is straightforward. The grid from the previous chapter will be handy for this. It's wise to use a pencil for the first rough draft. I use a straight edge to get the vertical lines correct, but ink them in free-hand. You might try this method. To rule lines directly with a pen makes the drawing appear much too clean cut. The hand-made stones and slabs are not perfectly square anyway.

Move about your village

You will find it useful to wander all around a village before you choose your precise subject. Different van-tage points can dramatically alter the possibilities for a drawing.

Another part of Dent is shown in the sketch above. The near cottage had a rounded corner wall. I suggested the cobbled street by drawing patches of elliptical marks and small dashes. I didn't attempt to cover all the ground in the same way, as this would probably have made the finished picture too dark. The houses here, compared to those in a city, are quite small. See how my building stones are drawn. Some I have hatched diagonally, others I have marked with curved dashes.

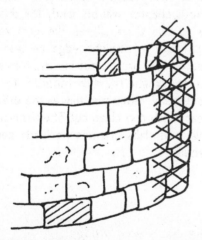

The detail above shows how I have created shadow, by loosely cross-hatching over the top of the sketched stones.

I put in the lady to give interest and to show scale. I have drawn her slightly larger above to help you see her proportions. If you can get her basic shape right then she's easy to draw.

A bird's-eye view

Roof-top scenes can make attractive drawings. I have seen many over the years: London, Paris, Venice and other cities provide the roof-top artist with endless choice. You might like to try some of your own — but be careful how you scramble about high up to gain the best view! It may be safer for you to start off by copying one of mine.

When I stayed in Bourton-on-the-Water, in the Cotswolds, I had a wonderful bird's-eye view of the buildings standing opposite to the one I was in. I decided to draw the view as it was, rather than to shift some of the trees away.

This sketch was made quite small, on an A5 pad. I used a 0.5 pen to do a controlled scribble with lots of dots for the trees, but switched to a size 0.1 pen for the buildings.

Challenge yourself

Now that you can draw pretty well, it's time to challenge yourself — you will have no new problems with copying these slightly harder examples. Have patience and take your time.

When I looked at this little valley in Northumberland I saw that it had a natural composition. Note the way the dry stone wall follows the contours of the slopes. The shadow cast by the tree in the centre also helps to suggest the form of the land, as does the line of fence posts. The clouds were first put in with pencil and then the horizontal sky lines were inked up to these outlines. Distant fells are recorded by light, broken lines. Shrubs and trees have been drawn with dot stipple.

The scene above seemed to be waiting for an artist to sketch! I drew the dense shadows in the water with a controlled scribble which tapered off into diagonal strokes to show ripples. Deep shade on the near wall was made by cross-hatching. This one should be no trouble to copy.

The scene below depicts a lane on the well-kept estate of the Duke of Northumberland. I didn't meet the Duke or find a tea room during my visit but the marvellous scenes made up for this! This is really a study of simple shading and dot stipple which you will manage easily.

On the right is my drawing of the hermit's cave on the same estate. It has a statue outside of the late tenant — whom I named Kermit! It's not really a landscape but I thought it would be a good exercise for you to do. I drew this first in pencil, then I began inking in the cave with a small brush and drawing ink. The dark coloured leafy moss above the cave I did with a controlled scribble. I used dots and dashes with a size 0.5 pen to show beech masts scattered around the entrance. The rock ledge, just inside the cave opening, I cross-hatched to create depth and suggest deep shadow. That is all there is to producing this unusual illustration. Give it a go.

On the left is Lindisfarne Castle, which is perched on a pinnacle of rugged rock that juts through folds of grass. I drew the rock with a kind of controlled scribble made up of squiggly lines and then shaded them over where the shadows were. You could get 'writer's' cramp putting in all the dot stipple in this example! I saw many visitors when I was there but just drew two of them to give an idea of scale. While working on this sketch I also had the pleasure of drawing baby rabbits who popped out within a pace of where I was. They seemed interested in what I was doing!

The sketch above, of a waterfall in bonny Scotland, is the last drawing for you to copy. See how dense cross-hatching on rocks helps to emphasise water. Light areas left blank in the water suggest the foaming rush, cascading down the rocks. Note how shading shows through the tree on the right of the scene. This is an easy drawing but it does take time. I'm sure you will manage it.

Venture forth

Now it's time for you to venture forth and prove to all that you are an artist. You may not have to go far. You could find a picture waiting to be drawn near to where you live — perhaps your local park?

You will need the right clothes and footwear for outdoor work. A hat with a brim or peak is a must — especially in bright light. When it's cold a hat helps to retain body warmth. Waterproofs are a good idea. You can carry your drawing gear in a small rucksack, travel bag or case. A folding stool or foam plastic mat to sit on will be useful. Take enough food and drink to sustain you — important if there isn't a tea room handy. If you take along this book you will never be stuck for information about what technique to use. Good luck!

RIGHT WAY
PUBLISHING POLICY

HOW WE SELECT TITLES

RIGHT WAY consider carefully every deserving manuscript. Where an author is an authority on his subject but an inexperienced writer, we provide first-class editorial help. The standards we set make sure that every **RIGHT WAY** book is practical, easy to understand, concise, informative and delightful to read. Our specialist artists are skilled at creating simple illustrations which augment the text wherever necessary.

CONSISTENT QUALITY

At every reprint our books are updated where appropriate, giving our authors the opportunity to include new information.

FAST DELIVERY

We sell **RIGHT WAY** books to the best bookshops throughout the world. It may be that your bookseller has run out of stock of a particular title. If so, he can order more from us at any time – we have a fine reputation for "same day" despatch, and we supply any order, however small (even a single copy), to any bookseller who has an account with us. We prefer you to buy from your bookseller, as this reminds him of the strong underlying public demand for **RIGHT WAY** books. However, you can order direct from us by post or by phone with a credit card.

FREE

If you would like an up-to-date list of all **RIGHT WAY** titles currently available, please send a stamped self-addressed envelope to

ELLIOT RIGHT WAY BOOKS, BRIGHTON ROAD, LOWER KINGSWOOD, TADWORTH, SURREY, KT20 6TD, U.K.

or visit our website at www.right-way.co.uk